𝕿𝖍𝖊 𝕾𝖙𝖆𝖗, 𝕿𝖍𝖊 𝕾𝖆𝖎𝖓𝖙 𝕬𝖓𝖉 𝕿𝖍𝖊 𝕮𝖎𝖙𝖞

How Sam Brannan's Newspaper Heralded The Gold Rush and Created San Francisco

Also by the Author

BADASS LAWMAN: Guns, Gangs and the Sheriff Who Tamed the Golden State (2022)

THAT PIRATE, BOUCHARD: Revolutions, Redemption and the Plunder of Old California (2023)

The Star, The Saint And The City

How Sam Brannan's Newspaper Heralded The Gold Rush and Created San Francisco

William Briggs

Published by
William Briggs
Morgan Hill, CA 95037
4957_4

ISBN 978-1-956785-56-2

*For Journalists Everywhere,
Saints and Sinners Alike*

Table of Contents

Foreword

Good feature writing focuses on a person, place or thing. This nonfiction historical work, *The Star, The Saint and The City*, combines all three elements into a highly readable chronicle of San Francisco's colorful past.

The *person* is the "Saint," Sam Brannan, a 19th century Mormon Church leader who established the first community of Latter-Day Saints on the West Coast. As one of San Francisco's earliest venture capitalists, he became the state's first millionaire, only to die in poverty and relative historical obscurity.

The *place,* "The City," is a dead giveaway for anyone living in the region. Everyone in northern California knows "The City" is shorthand for San Francisco. When Brannan first arrived, San Francisco didn't exist yet. It was a sleepy hamlet alongside the bay. He would change that.

The *"thing"* was Brannan's *The California Star*, the first newspaper in San Francisco history. Though short-lived, when it broke the news of the discovery of gold in California, it was perhaps the single most important "scoop" in the state's journalistic history, with the greatest impact on what would become the Golden State.

Weaving these three themes together yields a compelling storyline with a unique perspective into the period just prior to the discovery of gold in 1848. The resulting Gold Rush, which

Brannan played a key role in promoting, would dramatically transform him, local journalism and the history of the West – all within a few short years. With solid research and an entertaining style, author Bill Briggs has tied up the loose ends of The City's origins and brought back to life a largely forgotten page of early San Francisco history.

During my own 30-year career as a northern California journalist, I developed a passion for the history of our region. For a time, I was editor of California's oldest weekly newspaper, *The Mountain Messenger*, in Downieville, in the Sierra foothills. On breaks at night, while putting the paper to bed, I'd read stories in the old bound copies of those wild, early Gold Rush Days.

Bill and I had known each other since my days teaching at City College of San Francisco and Bill was Director of the School of Journalism at San Jose State University, where he once tried to hire me. So, when Bill asked me to write a foreword for this book, I recognized we shared more than a passing interest in journalism, its history and the stories from California's past.

Bill seemed particularly interested in my relationship with San Francisco. Being a fifth generation native myself, I felt steeped in The City's cultural and natural history, geography, geology and politics. That assumption was shattered, however, when I walked every street in San Francisco – all 2,612 of them – and wrote a series of stories as a reporter for the *San Francisco Chronicle*. I realized how little I knew of my hometown. After completing my walk-about, research and articles, I got a much better sense of the place now.

But I still knew little of Sam Brannan, his fledgling newspaper, *The California Star,* and its role in shaping my hometown's future. It's important to point out that newspapers are not only the first draft of history, but also they often are the only form of information available to local communities. To learn more, we took a nine mile walk through San Francisco's Financial District and Chinatown, looking for reminders of what Brannan found when he arrived at Yerba Buena in 1846.

Big events were already unfolding. A few months earlier, Americans at Sonoma and Sacramento had launched the Bear Flag Revolt and proclaimed California independent. Soon the United States had declared war against Mexico and annexed Alta California. Within months of arrival, Brannan chaired a relief effort for the stranded Donner Party, gold was discovered on the American River, the Gold Rush ensued, and California was admitted to the union by 1850. Yerba Buena was renamed San Francisco and its population surged from a few hundred to nearly 30,000. Now San Francisco boasts a population of more than 800,000. Today, those wind-swept sand dunes around Portsmouth Square are buried beneath asphalt, concrete, and stucco and much of the bay shoreline filled in with abandoned ships and mounds of excavated sand from leveled hills.

As we walked the streets of San Francisco, searching for clues, we realized Sam Brannan's newspaper, *The California Star,* was a "flash in the pan," a Gold Rush expression meaning a brief success that didn't "pan out". The paper shut down within a year and a half when all its staff headed for the gold fields, like everyone else in San Francisco. But the paper's timing was perfect. It would herald the Gold Rush.

Although Brannan left a huge imprint on San Francisco and California history, his accomplishments have faded with time, like gold dust in the wind. The Gold Rush had put San Francisco and its first newspaper on the map, and then left the fledgling *California Star* high and dry, like the abandoned sailing ships in Yerba Buena Cove.

Whether you're passionate or even mildly interested in San Francisco and California history, you'll find this book informative, and come away with a better understanding of how this place we call home became what it is today. You may have a hard time putting this volume down, but after turning its pages, you'll want to earmark some of its passages and then hit the streets yourself to retrace some of Sam Brannan's first footsteps in a hamlet called Yerba Buena, which became one of the most popular and prosperous places on the planet.

Like San Francisco historian Daniel Bacon once told me: *"Sometimes you can just stand on a street corner and feel the history all around you."*

Tom Graham
Sacramento, California
2023

Preface

In the 1936 movie, *San Francisco,* Jeanette MacDonald stands among the rubble of the great 1906 San Francisco earthquake and sings a love song to the devastated city. It became an anthem:

> *"San Fran-cisco*
> *Open your golden gate.*
> *You let no stranger wait outside your door."*

I'm a native San Franciscan. I call it "The City" and bristle when someone refers to it as "Frisco." I've experienced many of the world's great cities. San Francisco remains unique. It truly is, as Bohemian poet George Sterling called it, *"The Cool, Gray City of Love."*

My San Francisco roots go deep. My great-grandfather, a Swiss immigrant, became the powerful secretary of the Brewery Workers Union there. My grandfather ran saloons before, during and after Prohibition. My grandmother camped out in Golden Gate Park after the earthquake and fire of 1906. Her brother survived the horrific glass works roof collapse during the 1900 Stanford-California football game and, with a shattered right elbow, became an uncommon left-handed semi-pro baseball second baseman. My mother was one of The City's first women pharmacists. My parents married at Grace Cathedral before my father shipped out with the Navy to Guadalcanal during World War II. I was born at St. Francis

Hospital in the baby-boom shortly after all those servicemen sailed back home through the welcoming arms of the Golden Gate.

Growing up on the San Francisco Peninsula, The City was always a magnet: Playland at the Beach, the Zoo, the Wharf, hip North Beach, naughty Broadway, exotic Chinatown. Four thousand restaurants – all good. Folk singers at the *Purple Onion* and up-and-coming stars at the *hungry i.* Jazz at *Basin Street* and the *Black Hawk*. And later the rock scene with the Airplane, Dead and Janis. The Avalon, Fillmore and free concerts in Golden Gate Park. Beats, hippies, gays, straights, all the ethnicities and quirky neighborhoods on all those hills – it all seemed to fit together.

As kids, hungry for sports, we could watch the transplanted (from New York) Giants play at old Seals Stadium – *Say Hey, Willie Mays;* catch the 49ers at Kezar Stadium, where the seagulls outnumbered the fans and the fog was so thick it obscured half the field; or follow the (then San Francisco) Warriors and watch epic duels between Wilt Chamberlain and Bill Russell, who had starred locally at USF.

The local media was an important part of The City. *KSFO* billed itself as the "World's Greatest Radio Station," and, anchored by local legend Don Sherwood, it may have been. T*he Chronicle* and *Examiner* were lively rivals, and the incomparable columnist Herb Caen wrote for them both (My mother would later clip Caen's columns and send them to me in Vietnam). My first job, at age 10, was as a newspaper carrier. I delivered the *San Francisco News,* as well as the pink *Call Bulletin,* and after they merged, I carried the *S.F. News-*

Call. Each afternoon I'd come home from school, pick up my bundle of papers and box-fold them into little square packages that I could sling from my bike and hit the customers' porches without stopping. It taught me work ethic, money management and customer service. Once a customer tipped me with a kitten. But not only did I deliver the papers – rain or shine – but also, I read them. Comics, sports, news and editorials. I was addicted to news.

After college and discharge from the Army, I studied journalism and began writing for newspapers, magazines, radio and cable television, followed by stints in advertising and public relations; all before completing a doctorate at USF and moving into a three-decade career in academe, teaching communications and administering two of the most respected university journalism programs in the West. I particularly enjoyed teaching History of American Media, combining my undergraduate training in historiography with my journalism experience.

In retirement, I have returned to my first love of history. *The Star, The Saint and The City,* completes what I call my Golden State trilogy of less-well-known stories from California's colorful past. San Francisco history and journalism here have come full circle. I've been able to tell the story of one of California's most vibrant, influential and outrageous figures of the 19th century, Samuel Brannan, set against the tapestry of the California Gold Rush and the evolution of what became the California of today. And this work is also an origin story of a newspaper and of a city. Few newspapers have ever had such a seismic impact as kick-starting the Gold Rush. Few civic births have been as dramatic and consequential as the overnight transformation of Yerba Buena into San Francisco.

In 4th grade, California social studies curriculum covers state history. Students learn about the Spanish explorers, the *padres* who founded the missions, and the Gold Rush. Missing from my lessons were accounts of the brutal treatment of the Native Americans under the mission system or the enormous role played by Mormon pioneers in opening California. Mentions of Sam Brannan were few. I can only speculate as to why these omissions occurred. I've tried to make sure these stories get told as well. It's not revisionist history nor political correctness; rather it's just more complete, more honest, better history.

Although I have some Mormon ancestry, I am not a Mormon and was not raised in that religious tradition. Thus, I tread lightly when it comes to writing about that often-misunderstood religion. I have tried to learn enough about that church's history to further my narrative and understand how or why religious beliefs motivated people or influenced events. Historians build their stories on a foundation of available fact. Facts, as used in a religious context, are often rooted in faith, a different case altogether. Suffice to follow the historical trail of evidence. I'll leave the theological discussions to others. Any misstatements of fact or misrepresentations of belief are this author's sole responsibility.

A word about word usage. The religion central to our story is The Church of Jesus Christ of Latter-Day Saints, a lengthy and somewhat awkward title, particularly when used repeatedly. The Church officially discourages the term

"Mormon" and the abbreviation "LDS", preferring "Saints," "Latter-Day Saints" and "Church of Jesus Christ." An exception would be a historical proper name such as the "Mormon Battalion." The term "Mormon" was taken in early times from *The Book of Mormon* and often used by non-believers with negative connotations. But even the Church recognizes that after nearly two centuries of common use and universal recognition of the term "Mormon," it is futile, and possibly counter-productive, to fight its use. Unbound by religious rules, in the interest of brevity, clarity and greater reader comprehension, I have respectfully chosen to retain use of the word "Mormon" as well as "Saints" to describe the religion and its followers. As shorthand for the institutional title, I've employed "the Church," as a capitalized proper name, much as might be used to describe specific reference to the Roman Catholic Church or Church of England as "the Church." The word "gentile" originally referred to anyone not a Jew. The word was appropriated by the Latter-Day Saints to forge a spiritual, if not genetic, connection with the ancient Tribes of Israel and used to mean anyone not of the Latter-Day Saint faith. That poses an interesting conundrum: Are Jews therefore gentiles? Regardless, for our story, "gentile" is a generic term referring to anyone outside the faith, rather than any specific race, ethnicity or religion.

Much conversation of late has bemoaned San Francisco's sale of its soul. The influx of technology start-ups, fueled by venture capital, Red Bull and greed, created a real estate bubble only the newly rich or long-time residents could afford. When the bubble burst, it left behind gentrified neighborhoods and an urban core of high-priced, vacant office towers, while legions of the unhoused occupied the streets outside. Some major retail outlets have opted out of the downtown core. Perception of street crime and public drug use has become the reality. Sadly, many out-of-town visitors and out-of-state investors are no longer drawn to The City by the Bay. Many of the young, the colorful, the creative who gave San Francisco its vibe have abandoned The City. In 2022, San Francisco experienced a population decline of an estimated 60,000. (Several other Bay Area cities also have experienced declining population, though not as dramatic.) This exodus results in reduced business and property tax revenue, restricting The City's ability to provide services. In turn, this could cause more flight in what *The San Francisco Chronicle* has dubbed *"the doom loop."* But every time after fire has destroyed The City; every time an earthquake has crumbled it; after vigilantism, corruption, political assassinations, AIDS epidemic or invasion of flower children have rocked San Francisco, it has recalibrated and renewed to welcome the stranger, entice the opportunist, seduce the dreamer. Not surprising. It's encoded in The City's DNA, from birth parents who were religious refugees, adventurers and half-crazed seekers of gold.

Like peeling layers of an onion, our story begins with a paragraph, buried within an article, hidden on the inside page of an obscure newspaper start-up called *The California Star*. It changed the world.

William Briggs
Morgan Hill, California
2023

Introduction

"The newspaper is a greater treasure to people than uncounted millions in gold."

–Henry Ward Beecher,
Proverbs from Plymouth Pulpit, 1887
(Wm. Drysdale ed.)

One summer morning in August 1848, a staff reporter at the *New York Herald* confronted a stack of newspapers which had recently arrived from parts of the country far afield. He sighed as he picked through the papers. His job was to glean stories from other newspapers to help fill the pages of the *Herald.* This was not the glamorous side of journalism; not the rush of covering a salacious murder nor the drama of reporting a tenement fire. But his newspaper required content to satisfy the readers whose eyeballs justified the support of the advertisers. So much of all this local journalism from around the country was either poorly written or badly reported and thus unusable. Not up to New York standards certainly. And here was a newspaper from somewhere in the far west, San Francisco. Might as well be from the far side of the moon. As the reporter started mining the lunar broadsheet for nuggets of news, he had no idea that he was about to strike a nugget of gold.

By the 19th century, newspapers had become an integral part of the American fabric. It was part of the democratizing

1

process famously noted by de Tocqueville. As the country moved westward, printing presses accompanied the pioneers. Most communities of any size had a paper and citizens came to depend upon them. However, in all but the large cities, few newspapers had the resources to extensively cover even local news. In many communities the publisher also doubled as beat reporter, writer, editor, typesetter, printer, distributor, advertising salesman (yes, they were almost always men), bookkeeper and janitor. In addition, to make ends meet, most papers also served as commercial printers for local businesses or government. From colonial times forward, newspapers borrowed stories from other papers to fill their own editions.

In the 19th century, American journalism had largely freed itself from the partisan patronage of political parties and replaced it with an advertising-driven business model: the more attractive the product, the more subscribers; the more customers, the more attractive to advertisers and the higher the advertising revenue; the more revenue, the bigger the product, which attracted even more readers and even higher advertising rates, and so on. With profitability came greater reach, more frequency of publication, technological improvements and even additional staff.[1]

However, this drive for more news, greater circulation and higher profits was like feeding a beast which could never be satisfied. In the early decades of the 19th century there existed no news syndicates, wire services, foreign correspondents, professional researchers nor a public relations industry providing a steady diet of ready-to-print press materials. Instead publishing entrepreneurs relied on the symbiotic sharing of news and information to supplement their own efforts. While larger metropolitan newspapers eventually became big enough to treat their own reporting as exclusive and compete with each other, even papers like the *New York Herald* had to keep the beast fed.

The *New York Herald* had been started on a shoestring in 1835 by James Gordon Bennett, whose biting style and aggressive independence made him very unpopular with the business and political elite. But his public embrace of objectivity and his take-no-prisoners approach to news made him one of the earliest investigative reporters. He expanded news coverage and departmentalized popular topics such as sports, entertainment, business and national news. He was an early adopter of telegraph technology in sourcing and disseminating the news and his circulation figures eventually outpaced all his New York competitors. He had a nose for news and would know a scoop when he encountered it.

Thus, the *Herald* reporter began combing through *The California Star* datelined April 1, 1848. The paper was a special edition of the weekly published in San Francisco by Samuel Brannan and edited by Edward C. Kemble and designed to extoll the virtues of far-off California in order to attract more immigration to the region recently annexed by the United States from Mexico. Scanning through columns of small-point type, buried in the fourth paragraph of the fourth column on the fourth page in an article headlined *The Great Sacramento Valley,* he came across this matter-of-fact report:

> *"It* [the Sacramento Valley] *has a mine of gold and a probable estimate of its magnitude cannot be derived from any information we have received. It was discovered in December last on the south*

branch of the American Fork, in a range of low hills forming the base of Sierra Nevada distant 30 miles from New Helvetia."[2]

In his re-write, the east coast reporter added:

"...without allowing any golden hopes to puzzle my prophetic vision for the future, I would predict for California a Peruvian harvest of the precious metals, as soon as a sufficiency of miners can be obtained."[3]

On August 19, 1848, *Bennett* ran the story on page one under the headline *"Gold Discovered in California."* The word was out; the genie had escaped the bottle. Other papers would soon also receive a copy of *The Star* or reprint from the *New York Herald.* Sam Brannan's effort to encourage more settlement in California had, in fact, launched the greatest population migration in American – and possibly the world's – history.

Notes:

1. This advertising-based business model remains the foundation for most media companies in capitalist democracies. However, in the 21st century, newspapers have generally suffered decline in readership and revenue as advertisers have gravitated to digital platforms and the reading public increasingly has turned to various electronic outlets for their news, or to social media. Local journalism, arguably the most important, has been particularly hard hit by this trend.

2. The Sacramento Valley," *The California Star,* vol. II, No. 13, April 1, 1848. In fact, the discovery of gold was in January 1848, not the previous December. New Helvetia refers to Sutter's Fort, established by Swiss immigrant John Sutter along the Sacramento River.

3. "Gold Discovered in California," *The New York Herald,* Aug. 19, 1848.

William Briggs

Chapter 1
The Great Bay

"I'm sittin' on the dock of the bay
Watchin' the tide roll away"

–Otis Redding/Steve Cropper
Dock of the Bay, 1967

Very long ago, between one and two hundred million years, the plates sliding on the earth's molten crust were working hard. The Pacific Plate was grinding against the North American Plate and scraping up enough material from the sea floor to add hundreds of square miles of real estate to the California coast. In a process called subduction, the Pacific Plate pushed under the continent and uplifted the majestic Sierra Nevada cordillera and the lesser coastal mountain ridges. In the process, the foothills of the Sierra were studded with rich veins of a golden metal, which one day would transform California.

The land between the mountain chains became a vast inland sea, which eventually receded, creating the fertile Central Valley and carving out the basin that would become San Francisco Bay. With the melting of glaciers at the end of the last great ice age, about 10,000 years ago, the sea levels rose, and a small section of the coastal range collapsed, allowing seawater to surge in through what we now call the

Golden Gate. Sea water mixed with the drainage of two great rivers, the Sacramento and the San Joaquín, in three adjoining bays, forming a huge new bay, destined to become one of the world's great natural harbors. As sea level rise slowed, sand blew in from the exposed coastal beaches, building up huge sand dunes.

About 13,000 years ago – yesterday in geological time – humans from Asia crossed to North America by a land bridge and began migrating southward, eventually populating both American continents from Alaska to Patagonia. For millennia, subsets of some fifty Native American tribes, about a third of all inhabitants of the Americas, lived in harmony with nature in the area we now call California. These included the groups known collectively as Miwok north of the bay and Ohlone in the south bay region, who thrived in the benign weather and natural bounty of marshlands, mudflats, valleys and hills ringing the bay and the adjacent coastal environment. They called their place *Yelamu*. This ancestral way of life would be interrupted and ended by the arrival of Europeans looking for a bay.

By the end of the 15th century of the common era, European states, principally the seafaring nations of Spain and Portugal, were poised to explore beyond their known world in search of the riches of the Indies, Cathay and Cipango (Spice Islands, China and Japan). In 1494, the Roman Catholic pope partitioned the new world between the two rival, but both Catholic, countries of Spain and Portugal with the Treaty of Tordesillas. Portugal would own eastward routes of exploration through the Atlantic and Indian Oceans; Spain fell heir to the Americas (except Brazil) and westward across the Pacific.

After Vasco de Gama sailed around the African cape to India, the Portuguese navigator Ferdinand Magellan, sailing for Spain, pushed on to the Philippines, successfully completing the first circumnavigation of the globe in 1522 (though he lost his life before completing the voyage himself). Trying to find a route to Asia, Columbus had been blocked by two entire continents. To more readily access the riches of Asia, Spain found it necessary to conquer and colonize the Americas which stood between it and the Far East. This they accomplished in short order and with bloody efficiency, with the conquest of the Aztec Empire in Mexico by Hernán Cortés (1519-21), followed soon by the conquistador Francisco Pizarro's ruthless subjugation of the Incas in Peru (1532).

Popular conjecture held that there were many islands between America and Cipango and that California was an island of riches, ruled by a warrior queen called Calafia, heroine of a popular 1510 epic Spanish chivalric novel. The name, itself, may have derived from the Arabic, *khalifa* (caliph or leader), well-known to Spaniards who had only recently expelled the Moors from Spain after centuries of Muslim rule. By the time Spaniards explored Baja (lower) California and determined it to be a peninsula rather than an island, and that it extended from Alta (upper) California on the northern continent, the name was in common usage. Nevertheless, the myth that California was an island was perpetuated by mapmakers well into the 17th century.

Having established and secured ports on the west coast of both Mexico and South America, within a generation Spain began an annual trade with the Philippines. By 1565, Miguel Lopez de Legazpi had established a permanent Spanish colony in Manila. Enormous ships, known as Manila galleons, would sail from Acapulco, Mexico, their holds full of Mexican and South American gold and silver, and follow the eastward winds and currents near the equator across the Pacific to Asia. Trading the precious metals for rare spices, porcelain, silk and other commodities coveted by Europeans, these galleons would seek the northerly, clockwise Japanese current that would bring the ships back to North America. The entire trip could take as long as eight months of hard sailing. Success was uncertain and ships were lost at sea, or even to pirates. By the time galleons arrived off California they were often in serious need of repair, before the final journey down the coast of North America to Acapulco. To address this issue and prevent further loss of cargoes, crews and ships, the Spanish admiralty called for establishment of a safe, deep-water harbor on the California coast. However, San Francisco Bay was not ready to be discovered.

Hoping to discover the Straits of Anián, the fabled sea road between the Pacific and the Atlantic Oceans, as well as to deny the Portuguese western access to the Spice Islands and Philippines, in 1542, the Viceroy of New Spain (modern Mexico, California and much of the current southwestern United States) commissioned Juan Rodriguez Cabrillo to explore the California coast. Cabrillo was an experienced Spanish admiral who had participated in the conquest of the Aztecs with Cortés, where he had notoriously caulked his ships with the rendered fat of his human victims. Cabrillo sailed north to the California Channel Islands, then, buffeted by fierce storms, reached the cape just north of San Francisco Bay, called Point Reyes, before tuning back. Whether by fog or by sailing too far from shore to observe, Cabrillo twice had missed the obscured entrance to the great bay, though he did discover the deep-water bay at Monterey a short distance to the south.

Soon, other nations began challenging Spain's dominance of the seas. The appearance of English privateers in Spanish waters off the coast of Spanish America heightened the need to establish a safe anchorage for the returning galleons. Francis Drake and Thomas Cavendish, a pair of greatly feared English privateers, known as *Sea Dogs,* were essentially pirates sailing with a governmental commission to harass enemy targets at sea. They had sailed from England, successfully navigated the Straits of Magellan around Cape Horn and were plundering the ports along the Pacific coast of South America and attacking Spanish shipping. With his ship's hold full of looted treasure, Drake sailed north along the coast in search of what he called the Northwest Passage which he hoped would take him back to England, thus avoiding sailing back through South American waters where the Spanish would certainly be waiting for revenge. However, the Arctic conditions of the North Pacific forced Drake to turn back. Drake was desperate for a place to repair his badly leaking and weather-beaten ship, the *Golden Hinde.*

Historians differ on where Drake put ashore, but many agree it was in the south-facing lee of Point Reyes, today called Drake's Bay, within only a few miles of San Francisco's great bay. Here the intrepid Englishman rested his crew, careening his ship, that is beaching the vessel and rolling it first to one side and then the other, to repair the hull and clean away algae, seaweed, barnacles and wood boring worms below the water line, and recaulk the hull – a complex process. There the

English interacted with the friendly indigenous Miwok natives. Reminded of the white cliffs of his homeland, Drake claimed the land for England, calling it *Nova Albion,* a name English language maps would use in preference to *California* for the next couple of centuries. After several weeks, Drake sailed from California, eastward across the Pacific, eventually completing only the second circumnavigation of the globe and receiving a royal hero's reception by Queen Elizabeth I, though details of his exploration of the California coast were kept secret from the Spanish. English claims on California would surface sporadically over the next centuries, but no English colonization was ever undertaken. San Francisco Bay remained unknown.

In July 1595, a Manila galleon, on return from Asia, explored the California coast as it sailed southward. It's captain, Sebastían Rodriguez Cermeño, anchored at Drake's Bay off Point Reyes. He named the bay *Puerto y Bahia de San Francisco* (this was not the bay of that same name we know today but rather Drake's Bay). After storms wrecked his ship, the crew attempted to sail back to New Spain (Mexico) in a small boat, yet even hugging the coastline, still failed to notice the entrance to the great bay. Cermeño was followed seven years later by Sebastían Vizcaíno. Though his expedition also ended in disaster and death of most of his crew, he produced the first detailed maps of the California coast, as far north as the mouth of the Columbia River. The maps indicate an indentation identified only as *Enseñada Grande* (Great Cove).[1] He had seen the opening of the Golden Gate, though never sailed inside nor realized the bay's great size. His maps remained a Spanish state secret for two centuries and Spanish exploration would pause for almost that entire period.

When Spain ultimately rekindled interest in Alta California, it was not the search for a suitable, safe deep-water harbor for their galleons that spurred exploration and colonization. Rather, it was increased interest by other nations, notably Britain, in the northwest of America, and most particularly, the incursion of Russian fur traders and trappers south as far as the great bay at San Francisco. Spain had nervously watched Britain take over New France in North America and observed the rebellion growing in Britain's own North American colonies. Thus, the Spanish monarch, Carlos III, ordered a strategy for protecting the northern reaches of his far-flung colonial empire. The plan was to establish a chain of missions, supported and protected by strategically placed *presidios* (forts) along the coast of Alta California. The venture would begin at San Diego and then proceed north to Monterey and include the pious task of establishing a mission named for St. Francis of Assisi at Cermeño's Bahia de San Francisco.

Short of military personnel in *Nueva Espana* and equally strapped for cash, the government turned to the church for help. Spain considered itself the extension of the Catholic Church. The Catholic Jesuit order of priests had followed the Spanish conquistadors to the New World and quickly established missions in New Spain and South America, adapting Christianity to local cultures as much as theologically possible. Fearing their growing power and influence worldwide, the Spanish crown expelled the Jesuits from the Americas in 1767. They were replaced by the more conservative Franciscan order.

The reformist Visitor General in Mexico City, José de Gálvez, enlisted Franciscan friar Junipero Serra, recently arrived at San Blas in Baja California, to take over the former Jesuit operations and extend them into Alta California. *Father-Presidente* Serra had formed a partnership with Captain Gaspar de Portolá y Rovira, military governor in Baja California. Together they were charged by Gálvez to spread the Catholic faith, thwart foreign expansion and further Spanish claim to Alta California. The next foray into Alta California would be by land as well as sea. The expedition was plagued with problems from the start.

The land and sea parties embarked from Baja California to San Diego in July 1769. One ship never made it to the rendezvous and the land party, including Junipero Serra, was debilitated crossing the desert. Nevertheless, Portolá led the survivors north toward Monterey, hoping to establish a mission and *presidio* on the bay described by Vizcaíno. Reaching Monterey in October 1769, the Portolá expedition did not recognize that bay in the mist and pushed even farther north to the modern location of Pacifica. A month later, from a hilltop, Portolá's scouts spotted another bay and mistook it for Monterey; in fact, it was Bahia de San Francisco as called by Cermeño (modern Drake's Bay). Days later, on November 4th, the rest of the expedition arrived, and from an unobstructed coastal mountain vantage point on today's Sweeney Ridge, Sgt. José Francisco Ortega was likely the first Caucasian to finally gaze on the true expanse of San Francisco Bay, though the Portolá expedition never found its Golden Gate entrance.

Franciscan friar Juan Crespi, accompanying the expedition, recorded Portolá's impression of the bay as "*a great arm of the sea"* and large enough to contain all the *armadas* (fleets) of Europe.[2]

Meanwhile, Junipero Serra and accompanying Franciscans began the establishment of a chain of 21 missions in California, beginning at San Diego in 1769 and which ultimately would stretch to the northernmost Mission Solano by 1824. The role of the missions was to evangelize the indigenous natives into Christianity and become self-sufficient enterprises using the native workforce. Unlike the Jesuits, and backed by Spanish military might, the Franciscans tolerated no local beliefs and forced the local people toward Christian baptism and into hard manual labor. The treatment of the California Indians at the missions was often harsh and punishment could be brutal. European diseases added to the misery. The native population suffered greatly, and its numbers declined. Although the mission fathers remained fiercely loyal to the Spanish crown, the missions received very little support from New Spain.

The Spanish viceroy of New Spain, Antonio Bucareli, ordered a military reconnaissance of Alta California and in 1774, a troop under Captain Juan Bautista de Anza trekked as far north as Monterey. The following year he returned with a party of soldiers and civilians, including women and children, and a herd of cattle and horses and made the 1,500-mile journey to the shores of San Francisco Bay. At the same time, Juan Manuel de Ayala, onboard the *San Carlos*, sailed from Monterey in search of the great bay's mouth. On August 6, 1775, Ayala waited outside the Golden Gate before following a canoe through the choppy waters and anchoring first off modern Sausalito and then in a safe cove at an island he named Our Lady of the Angels, today's Angel Island. José de

Cañizares, pilot onboard the *San Carlos,* wrote a detailed report of his six-week-long reconnaissance into the bay, hoping to find a northern connection out to Drake's Bay. Though that connection did not exist, he did discover the mouth of the Sacramento River emptying into the bay and produced a map, later revised, that first used the name San Francisco Bay to describe the body of water inside the Golden Gate.

Months later, in the summer of 1776, as British colonial patriots argued over a Declaration of Independence in Philadelphia 3,000 miles away, the de Anza party completed the last leg from Monterey to the bay. One of de Anza's soldiers, Jose Joaquin Moraga, established *El Presidio Real de San Francisco* on the headlands overlooking the bay. Four *presidios* would be established in California, the others at Monterey, Santa Barbara and San Diego. These early Franciscans still hoped to establish their mission honoring St. Francis near the bay location Cermeño had originally named after their patron saint (in modern Marin County). However, unable to cross the Golden Gate opening and finding no circuitous route through the various bays and delta wetlands, the party settled on a site south of the Golden Gate. They began construction of a crude log and thatch church. Padre Francisco Palou, an associate of Father Serra, dedicated *Misión San Francisco de Assis,* named for the founder of the Franciscan order, on the bank of *Arroyo de Nuestra Señora de los Dolores* (Our Lady of Sorrows Creek) on October 9, 1776. Henceforth, the mission would be known as Mission Dolores. The seeds that would grow to become Yerba Buena, and blossom into San Francisco, had been planted.

Notes

1. Map from the Vizcaíno expedition, probably drawn by Antonio de la Ascensíon, and redrawn by Enrico Martínez, who was not on the voyage. In Derek Hayes, <u>Historic Atlas of California,</u> Oakland: University of California Press, 2007, p. 21.

2. Juan Crespi, Letter to Father Superior Juan Andres, Feb. 8, 1770, in *San Francisco Call,* vol. 106, no. 139, Oct. 17, 1909; California Digital Newspaper Collection, UCR Center for Bibliographical Studies and Research.

William Briggs

Chapter 2
Yerba Buena

"If California ever becomes a prosperous country, this bay will be the center of its prosperity."

– Richard Henry Dana,
Two Years Before the Mast, 1840

For more than two centuries, the Spanish had followed a policy of enforced isolation of Alta California, fearing encroachment of this remote, poorly defended outpost of empire by foreign rivals. Spain closed California ports to foreign shipping and allowed trading only with the mother country. By the early 19th century, Spain's global power was waning. South America and Mexico would soon fight for and eventually achieve independence. The annual supply ship to California from San Blas, Mexico had become unreliable and hostile Yuma Indians around the Colorado River had closed the land route into California from Mexico. In practice, the missions and *presidios* of Alta California increasingly depended upon smuggling and illicit trade with the outside world for all the necessities they could not provide for themselves. Foreign explorers and adventurers, trappers and traders, probed Alta California in ever-greater numbers. Aware of the fine harbor on San Francisco Bay, ships of other nations began to drop anchor in Yerba Buena Cove. The few Spanish soldiers at the *presidio* were unable – and probably unwilling – to stop them.

When the original de Anza expedition explored the San Francisco Peninsula, they found a trailing plant with mint-scented leaves growing in abundance.[1] The plant was similar to other plants found in Mexico and Central America, known as *yerba (*or *hierba) buena.* As José Moraga laid out an area to house workers midway between the *presidio* and the mission, he dubbed the area Yerba Buena. Decades later, as this camp site on the shore of the boat anchorage laid out a street grid and became a community, it retained the name Yerba Buena.

The first uninvited foreign visitor to the Spanish California coast was the esteemed British navigator Captain James Cook, on his third voyage of scientific exploration in the Pacific in 1777. On a secret mission to search for the long-sought Northwest Passage, Cook sailed north along the Oregon coast and into Alaskan waters, before turning back in fierce Arctic weather. While he did not visit San Francisco Bay, he was the first navigator to calculate longitude at sea, and thus the exact location of the California coast became public knowledge. Not to be out-done, the French sent Jean-Francois Galaup, Compte de Laperouse, to duplicate Cook's circumnavigation, systematically mapping the North American west coast in the process in 1785. Laperouse paid a visit to the *presidio* at Monterey and Mission San Carlos Borromeo, at Carmel, recording his observations of the inadequate state of defense and poor condition of the presidio and the maltreatment of the native people by the Franciscans.

The first non-Spanish ship to sail through the Golden Gate and anchor in Yerba Buena Cove was the *Discovery,* under British Captain George Vancouver in November 1792. Vancouver, who had earlier sailed with Captain Cook on two of Cook's voyages of discovery, was charting the northwest coast,[2] and received a warm welcome from the mission friars and the officers at the *presidio,* which he estimated to be inhabited by about 35 soldiers, their families and some Indian servants. Vancouver found the *presidio* to be unfinished and poorly constructed, a mud plaster wall about two hundred yards on a side enclosing a quadrangle and numerous thatched-roof huts. The mission complex was similarly constructed, but larger and more carefully completed. The serving Indians, Vancouver reported, had apparently been converted to Catholicism but demonstrated none of the attributes of western civilization. In summary, Vancouver wrote:

> *"Thus, at the expence* [sic] *of very little examination, though not without much disappointment, was our curiosity satisfied concerning the Spanish town and settlement of St. Francisco. Instead of finding a country tolerably well inhabited and far advanced in cultivation, if we except its natural pastures, the flocks of sheep and herds of cattle, there is not an object to indicate the most remote connection with any European, or other civilized nation."*[3]

Nevertheless, Vancouver found the harbor at Yerba Buena advantageous:

> *"The tides are there infinitely the most regular, and notwithstanding the bank of mud prevented our landing in some places, it does not extend all around the cove...The anchorage is more secure,*

by being completely land-locked and further removed from the ocean."[4]

Spain would soon relinquish interest in the farther northwest reaches of California and Oregon Territory. However, in part because of Vancouver's disdainful descriptions of Spanish California, Britain also ceased to pay much attention to the Pacific Northwest. Instead, explorers from new countries would find their way to California and began mapping the bay. Of immediate concern to Spain was the appearance of fur trappers from Alaska. The Russians were coming.

Russian fur trappers had crossed the Bering Sea to Alaska and established a base at New Archangel (modern Sitka). While animal fur had always been valued for its warmth, the soft, dense pelts of the sea otter were valued even more as a luxury status symbol, fetching high prices in Asian markets such as Canton, and justifying the long, perilous voyages across the Pacific. But harsh Arctic climate and hostile indigenous Tlingit natives made survival in Alaska difficult for the trappers. Death and disease drove the Russians southward on their quest for sea otter colonies to harvest.

The shifting European alliances in the wake of Napoleon Bonaparte's ambitions had brought Spain and Russia to the brink of war, though it took months for the news to reach California. And the decisive British defeat of the combined Spanish-French fleet at Trafalgar in 1805 rendered Spain even less able to defend its colonies in the Americas. Spain, via its viceroy in Mexico City, had admonished the governor of Alta California to receive any Russian visitors to Yerba Buena or Monterey with hospitality but prevent them from travel farther inland.

In March 1806 the Russian ship *Juno* sailed into San Francisco Bay. On board was Count Nicholas Rezanov, a courtier, diplomat and Imperial Russian spy, on a mission to secure food supplies for his starving comrades in Alaska but also to surreptitiously assess the strength of Spanish California. In a whirlwind period of two weeks, Rezanov both charmed and deceived the Spanish officials and mission friars, ingratiating himself into their community and persuading them that trade with Russia – Spanish prohibition notwithstanding – would be mutually beneficial. In a cynical diplomatic stroke to seal the deal, Rezanov proposed marriage to the infatuated Dona María de Concepcíon Marcela Arguello, called Conchita, the 15-year-old daughter of *Presidio Comandante* Don José Dario Arguello. Promising to return to his young bride-to-be, Rezanov journeyed back to Russia to present his findings to the Tsar, however he died enroute to St. Petersburg. His affair with Conchita sparked one of the earliest stories of tragic romance in California history. Despite this sad ending, Rezanov's dream of Russian colonization in California survived. A few years later, the Russian American Company established an agricultural outpost called Ross, only a few miles north of San Francisco Bay, to grow surplus of fruit and vegetables to supply the community at New Archangel. With Russia now established in Alta California, the two empires began a wary relationship, abutting each other and checkmating each other from further expansion.

Georg Heinrich von Langsdorff, a German-born naturalist and doctor who accompanied Rezanov, recorded his observations of the missions at San Francisco and also at San Jose in an 1812 book titled *Observations of a Journey Around the World.* Like Vancouver, he likened the *presidio* to a German farmstead. Von Langsdorff was particularly intrigued by the mission Indians:

> *"When it is considered that two or three padres and four or five soldiers keep in order a community of from a thousand to fifteen hundred rough and uncivilized men...it must be presumed that the cause is principally to be found in the mildness and forbearance with which they are treated...I must, however, also attribute the cause, in no small measure to the simplicity of these poor creatures, who, in stature no less than in mind, are certainly of a very inferior race of human beings."*[5]

Von Langsdorff's drawings provide the earliest, and best, representations of the California mission Indians in the early 19th century.

Russian ships began to visit Yerba Buena with greater frequency, along with ships of other nations, including Boston whalers flying the flag of the United States. In 1816, the Russian Otto von Kotzebue spent a month enjoying Spanish hospitality while exploring the bay. He returned a decade later and found conditions had deteriorated even further. By 1821, the Viceroyalty of New Spain (Mexico, California and much of Central America) had succeeded in throwing off the yoke of Spanish empire and declared independence. After a brief dictatorship, Mexico emerged as a republic, but not unlike its former Spanish overlord, found it increasingly difficult to support the missions of Alta California. By 1834, Mexico had secularized the missions and sold off the mission lands, creating enormous private *ranchos,* owned by a small number of wealthy families and retired military. Freed from the feudal mission system, the decimated native population ebbed into the landscape. Some of the missions struggled to remain active parish churches. However, the *ranchos* generally thrived, producing hides and tallow which were traded at California ports kept busy with regular foreign trade, including Yerba Buena.

Well into the 1800s there were only two officially designated *pueblos* in all of Alta California: El Pueblo de San José de Guadalupe, founded by José Joaquin Moraga in 1777; and El Pueblo de Nuestra Señora la Reina de los Angeles de Porciúncula (Pueblo of Our Lady Queen of the Angels of Porciúncula) named after the Porciúncula River where Fr. Juan Crespi founded a settlement in 1769.[6] There was nothing resembling a town at Yerba Buena. While the Franciscans and neophytes (converted Indians) occupied Mission Dolores and a small population of Spaniards and *Californios* (American-born of Spanish descent) lived at the *Presidio*, Yerba Buena was merely an anchorage for arriving ships.[7]

In 1822, a British sailor named William Richardson, a mate on board the whaler *Orion,* jumped ship at Yerba Buena and lived for several years at the *Presidio*. Fluent in Spanish and a convert to Catholicism, Richardson courted and married María Antonia Martínez, daughter of Ygnacio Martínez, *comandante* of the Presidio of San Francisco, in 1825. Richardson began a business of selling fresh water to visiting ships from a spring at Sausalito on the opposite bayside of the Golden Gate. In 1835, while waiting for a land claim to be approved, Richardson replaced his sailcloth tent at the *Presidio* with a two-story wooden building midway between the mission and the Presidio, up the required 200 *varas* (approximately 550 feet) from the water's edge at Yerba Buena Cove (today 823 Grant Ave. at Clay St.). He fronted his structure with a broad road connecting the trails to the mission and fort called *Calle de la Fundacion* (later Dupont and then Grant Avenue) and a plaza (later Portsmouth Square). The other streets in Yerba Buena would not be named until 1847. *Calle de la Fundacion* is generally considered the oldest street in San Francisco. This modest development marked the beginning of a trading post for arriving vessels. The Richardson family lived there alone for a year before they were joined by the village's second inhabitant, Jacob Leese. Richardson was given the title of Port Captain or harbormaster, a largely ceremonial position, though he piloted arriving ships and facilitated transfer of cargo from ship to shore and hides and tallow back into the holds of waiting ships. But on the Street of the Founding, this first Anglo settler had begun to build the city that would become San Francisco.

In 1826-27, the British naval geographer Frederick William Beechey spent seven weeks inside San Francisco Bay, creating charts that were used for decades. Beechey's maps switched the name Isla de Alcatraces (Islands of the Pelicans) from an island to later be renamed Yerba Buena to the rock that housed a Spanish prison and later an infamous U.S. penitentiary: Alcatraz. Beechey's account of his visit included this observation:

> *"Such of the seamen...made parties to visit the presidio and mission, where they found themselves welcome guests with the Spanish soldiers. These two places were the only buildings within miles of us, and they fortunately supplied just enough*

spirits to allow the people to enjoy themselves with their friends, without indulging in much excess – a very great advantage in a seaport."[8]

Beechey concludes,

"The more we became acquainted with the beautiful country around San Francisco, the more we were convinced that it possessed every requisite to render it a valuable appendage to Mexico...no fault can be found with its climate; its soil in general is fertile, it possesses forests of oak and pine convenient to building and contributing to the necessities of vessels, plains overrun with cattle, excellent ports and navigable rivers to facilitate inland communication. Possessing all these advantages, an industrious population alone seems requisite to withdraw it from obscurity in which it has so long slept under the indolence of the people and the jealous policy of the Spanish government."[9]

The settlement that developed around the *Presidio*, including Yerba Buena, had gained *pueblo* status from Mexican Governor José Figueroa in 1834, followed by election of an *ayuntamiento* (town council) and an *alcalde* (mayor or magistrate.) Plots of land were allocated for houses, gardens and pasture. A Swiss sailor with surveyor skills, named Jean Jacques Vioget, was commissioned to survey the *pueblo* in 1839. His map shows a dozen structures laid out on a grid of streets yet to be named.[7] But as late as 1841, there were only four permanent residents at Yerba Buena. William Richardson had finally had his land claim for the headlands across the

Golden Gate from the Presidio approved. He called it Rancho Sausalito and moved his family there in 1838, though he continued his role at Yerba Buena harbor.

Alta California was not a popular destination for immigration. Most of the landowners descended from the original Spanish explorers generations earlier. Military personnel at the *presidios* often chose to return to Mexico at retirement or the end of their enlistment. In order to populate the province, Mexico had relaxed its requirements for land ownership by foreign nationals who converted to Catholicism and applied for Mexican citizenship. This acted as a further buffer against the Russians who had moved as far south as the Santa Barbara Channel Islands hunting otters. However, depleted otter populations and the inability of Fort Ross to provide adequate surplus of foodstuffs to resupply Alaska forced a gradual withdrawal of the Russians from Alta California. Increasingly, the new threat to Mexican hegemony came from Anglo-Americans, sailors who jumped ship in the various ports, fur-trapping mountain men in greasy buckskins, or the slow trickle of settlers who were carving their way through snowy mountain passes in the Sierra into the foothills and valleys below. But for most Americans, California was still unknown. Awareness of the land west of the Sierra was heightened by a young law student-turned sailor named Richard Henry Dana who spent a couple years on a merchant ship plying the coastal waters and visiting California ports. For many, Dana's journal, published in 1840 as *Two Years Before the Mast,* was the first in-depth description of California. In time, it would become a classic.

In 1834, Dana had sailed from Boston around Cape Horn on board the ship *Pilgrim,* engaged in the trade of hides and tallow at the various California ports. In late 1835, aboard the ship *Alert,* he visited San Francisco Bay. His keen observations included prescient predictions of the harbor's future importance:

> *"Behind this* [the Presidio] *is the harbor in which trading vessels anchor, and near it, the mission of San Francisco, and a newly begun settlement, mostly of Yankee Californians, called Yerba Buena, which promises well. Here, at anchor, and the only vessel, was a brig under Russian colors, from Asitka, in Russian America, which had come down to winter, and to take in a supply of tallow and grain, great quantities of which latter article are raised in the missions at the head of the bay."*[10]

On December 27th, the *Alert* had completed its refitting, filled its hold with a cargo of hides, and set sail for the long journey that would ultimately return them to Boston. Dana recorded his last views of San Francisco Bay:

> *"We sailed down this magnificent bay with a light wind, the tide, which was running out, carrying us at the rate of four or five knots. It was a fine day; the first of entire sunshine we had had for more than a month. We passed directly under the high cliff on which the Presidio is built, and stood in the middle of the bay, from whence we could see small bays, making up into the interior, on every side; large and beautifully wooded islands; and the mouths of several small rivers. If California ever*

becomes a prosperous country, this bay will be the center of its prosperity. The abundance of wood and water, the extreme fertility of its shores, the excellence of its climate, which is as near to being perfect as any in the world, and its facilities for navigation, affording the best anchoraging [sic] *ground in the whole western coast of America, all fit in for a place of great importance; and, indeed, it has attracted much attention, the settlement of "Yerba Buena," where we lay at anchor, made chiefly by Americans and English, and which bids fair to become the most important trading place on the coast, at this time began to supply traders, Russian ships , and whalers, with their stores of wheat and frijoles* [beans].*"*[11]

Like the strong tides pulsing through the narrows of the Golden Gate, American expansion was accelerating, propelled by opportunity, greed and something called "Manifest Destiny." It would overcome Mexico's ability to resist the surge and it would transform a sleepy pueblo into an American city.

Notes

1. Yerba Buena, or *Clinopodium douglassii,* is an indigenous northern California plant related to spearmint.

2. Vancouver finally disproved the existence of a Northwest Passage.

3. George Vancouver, <u>A Voyage of Discovery to the North Pacific Ocean and Round the World, in which the Coast of North-West America has been carefully Examined and Accurately Surveyed; Undertaken by HIS MAJESTY'S Command, principally with a view to ascertain the existence of any navigable communication between the North Pacific and the north-Atlantic oceans and performed in the years 1790, 1791, 1792, 1793, 1794, and 1795 in the Discovery sloop of war and armed tender Chatham under the command of Captain George Vancouver</u>. Originally published in London for G.G. and J. Robinson and J. Edwards (1798); Milton Park, England: Routledge, 1984, W. Lamb (ed.).

4. <u>Ibid.</u>

5. Georg Heinrich von Langsdorff, <u>Voyages of the Travels in Various Parts of the World during the years 1803, 1804, 1805, 1806, and 1807,</u> London: Printed for Henry Colburn, 1814, in <u>The Rezanov Voyage to Nueva California,</u> The Russell California Reprints, San Francisco: Private Press of Thomas C. Russell, 1927, pp.61-62.

6. In time, both San Jose and Los Angeles would grow to become the 10th and 2nd largest U.S. cities.

7. Derek Hayes, <u>Historical Atlas of California,</u> Oakland: University of California Press, 2007, pp. 72-73.

8. Frederick William Beechey, <u>Narrative of a Voyage to the Pacific and Bering Strait</u>, in Peter Browning, <u>Yerba Buena, San Francisco. From the Beginning to the Gold Rush 1769-1849,</u> Lafayette CA: Great Books 1998, p. 84.

9. <u>Ibid</u>, p. 93.

10. Richard Henry Dana, Jr., <u>Two Years Before the Mast,</u> Chapter XXVI, originally published New York: Harper and Bros., 1840. Kindle electronic edition, non-paginated, 2022.

11. Ibid.

Chapter 3
Yankees

"It is the right of our manifest destiny to overspread and to possess the whole of the continent which Providence has given us for development of the great experiment of liberty and federated development of self government entrusted to us."
— John L. O'Sullivan,
New York Morning News, 1845

"Manifest Destiny was on the march, and it was unfortunate that Mexico stood in the path."
— Winston Churchill,
A History of the English-Speaking Peoples: The Great Democracies, 1958

At the same time Count Rezanov probed the San Francisco Bay with dreams of a Russian colony in California, an intrepid expedition of Americans prepared to leave their winter quarters near the mouth of the Colombia River on the Oregon coast and return east to report their findings to President Thomas Jefferson. In 1803, Jefferson, in a bold but controversial move, had purchased the Louisiana Territory from a cash-strapped Napoleon Bonaparte, doubling the size of the adolescent United States. Jefferson commissioned Meriwether Lewis and William Clark to explore this vast territory which was largely still unknown and populated by numerous tribes of Native American Indians. The publication of Lewis's journals in 1814 offered Americans the first authoritative glimpse of the rest of the continent.

Soon, rugged mountain trappers, such as the legendary Jedediah Smith, discovered the South Pass across the Continental Divide and opened trail routes west to Oregon Territory and south into California. Settlers followed the explorers. In 1841, the Bartleson-Bidwell party traversed the Sierra Nevada Mountains north of the Sonora Pass and followed the Stanislaus River into the San Joaquín Valley on the west of the Sierra. Lansford Hastings crossed the plains to Oregon in 1842 and then came south into California. He returned to Cincinnati and in 1845 published *Immigrants' Guide to Oregon and California* which trumpeted the virtues of California and would become a much-used travel reference. The previous year, the Stephens-Townsend-Murphy party of settlers, with help from Native American Paiute Indians, led by a chief named Truckee, negotiated a high mountain pass (now called Donner Pass) in the Sierra and followed the later-named Truckee River to become the first immigrant families to reach California by wagon. As an Irish Catholic, Martin Murphy was welcomed into Mexican society and became one of the great landowners of early California. Two years later, a combination of poor planning, bad timing and worse luck, doomed the Donner Party from Illinois. The ill-fated Donners had followed an erroneous short-cut across the Utah desert recommended by Lansford Hastings. The route actually proved longer and by the time the party sought another High Sierra pass, they found themselves caught in heavy winter snow and forced to resort to cannibalism for survival. The Donners lost half of their party before rescue, and the notoriety of their harrowing experience shocked the nation. Anglos and other foreigners still represented less than a tenth of the California population, but the Mexican government was becoming increasingly suspicious and resentful of their presence. The natural barriers of ocean and mountains had been breached. There was no way to stem the flow.

Forever seeking a buffer against the outsiders, first the Russians and next the Anglo-Americans, Mexico had readily formed an accommodation with a charismatic Swiss immigrant named Johann (John) Augustus Sutter. Sutter, leaving a trail of abandoned family, debt and legal problems behind in the old country in 1834, had made his way by his wits across North America and arrived in California by way of Fort Vancouver, Alaska and the Sandwich Islands (Hawai'i) by 1839. Sutter dreamed of an agricultural empire. With letters of reference and the force of his personality, he convinced Governor Juan Bautista Alvarado to let him establish a colony at the confluence of the Sacramento and American Rivers. Alvarado saw this move as a check against the Russians, American interlopers and even the troublesome Native American tribes. Allowing Sutter to become established in the delta hinterlands would also block the regional ambitions of the governor's uncle and chief rival, General Mariano Vallejo, whose cattle empire had already grown to hundreds of thousands of acres north of the Bay. With Alvarado's blessing, Sutter received Mexican citizenship in 1840 and was granted nearly 50,000 acres in 1841. Using Native American labor, he established a European-style fort and called his undertaking *Nueva Helvetia* – New Switzerland.

As California writer Max Arax described it:

"With land, labor and water, Sutter found he could be anything. He became the biggest farmer, storekeeper, innkeeper, distiller, miller, tanner, manufacturer, enslaver and liberator in California."[1]

Sutter's Fort became the commercial epicenter of California, and its master became one of the wealthiest, most respected Mexican citizens in Alta California. His fort covered almost an acre, surrounded by massive 20-foot adobe walls. Inside, the walls were lined with residences, storehouses and workshops including a distillery, bakery, gunsmith, carpentry shop and blacksmith. The large gate was closed at night and guarded by a pair of cannons. Outside the walls, living quarters, livestock corrals and various outbuildings sprung up. Sutter ruled his empire like a feudal lord. In 1841, Sutter purchased on credit for some $30,000, the entire holdings of Fort Ross from the Russians, who were abandoning their efforts in California. The Sutter empire continued its expansion. In return for service, he was granted even more land and controlled nearly 300 square miles of northern California wheat fields and ranch land. His cattle and sheep produced profitable hides and wool for trade.

Sutter's holdings became the first glimpse of civilization for weary explorers and immigrants trickling into California and Sutter played the generous host. The Stephens-Murphy immigrants restored themselves at Sutter's Fort and it served as the sanctuary for the desperate survivors of the Donner Party. However, by 1845, Sutter found himself drawn into a power struggle between rival Mexican political factions in the north and south that culminated in a brief civil war. As the locus of power shifted to a new governor in Los Angeles, Sutter found his own ambitions stymied. And into the confusion of the moment rode a pair of American figures with larger-than-life reputations: the soldier-explorer John C. Fremont and the legendary scout Christopher "Kit" Carson.

John Fremont had escaped a disadvantaged upbringing by securing a commission in the U.S. Army Corps of Topographical Engineers and became a skilled surveyor and frontiersman. In time he met, courted and married Jessie Benton, daughter of Missouri Senator Thomas Hart Benton. Senator Benton was a strong advocate of American expansion and secured appointment of Fremont to lead an expedition to survey and map the Oregon Trail. In 1844, Fremont and Carson became the first Anglos to cross the Sierra during winter. With help from his wife's skillful writing and editing, his report became widely read and Fremont's reputation as the heroic "Pathfinder" was established. Subsequent explorations into Oregon Territory and stealthily into Mexican Alta California, accompanied by Kit Carson, were similarly published and acclaimed. At Sutter's Fort, Fremont and company had been graciously entertained by the Swiss entrepreneur. However, their next meeting, in the spring of 1846, would turn Sutter's dreams sour and turn the fate of California upside down.

For many 19th century Americans, the country's experiment in democracy was validation that God had, in fact, smiled down on them as a chosen race. Thus, the idea of westward expansion was received with almost religious fervor. Other factors, such as population growth, the economic turn-down of the 1830s, the growing debate over the extension of slavery into new territories, lust for land, and wanderlust fueled by the writings of Fremont and others all contributed to the building momentum of migration west. The presence of Native Americans on the Great Plains or the fact that California and the southwest were already claimed by Mexico never deterred the expansionists. These were mere obstacles to be swept away. Racial, cultural and religious bigotry held sway. American exceptionalism ruled and possession of North America was after all America's divine destiny.

Author Simon Winchester wrote,

"...there were the Spanish [Mexican] *territories of Texas and California – millions upon millions of acres of land that looked at first quite freely available to any white man who wished to settle and prosper. If any native peoples...happened to stand in the way of this God-given right and duty, they should, said the settlers and speculators, be brusquely swept aside, all in the name of progress and the common good."* [2]

Remote and weakly administered by Mexico, California seemed ripe for taking. While Britain and France sniffed around the edges, the United States was much more overt, at first almost comically. In 1842, acting on rumors that Mexico and the United States were at war and that Mexico would rather cede California to Britain than see it taken by the Americans, Commodore Thomas ap Catesby Jones of the U.S. Navy's Pacific Squadron hurriedly sailed from Peru to Monterey and captured the Alta California capital in a coup. Soon learning that the war rumors were unfounded, the embarrassed commodore lowered the American flag and apologized to the Mexican governor in Los Angeles. But the would-be military occupation had come easily, and no one would sense California's vulnerability more than the Pathfinder, John Fremont. In ambition echoing Napoleon Bonaparte, Fremont saw conquest of California as the road to his political advancement and personal fortune.

Ironically, groups of influential *Californios,* perhaps convinced of the inevitable, and certainly disgruntled by Mexico's inability to govern California, were secretly seeking back-channel conversations with U.S. representatives about annexing California peacefully. Meanwhile in Washington D.C., politicians, led by Senator Benton, were beating the drums of Manifest Destiny. Soon they would also become the drums of war.

More than a decade earlier, in order to populate the northern reaches of Texas as a buffer against raiding Comanches, the government of Mexico had invited Americans to obtain land and settle there. Americans, mostly planters and farmers, but also land speculators, streamed in to occupy the rich, available land. The land was prime for raising cotton. Cotton growing required a large human workforce, and the southern planters brought their enslaved African Americans with them. However, the Mexican Constitution, which gave these *Texians* (Anglos in Texas) and *Tejanos* (Texans born of Mexican heritage) a large degree of governmental autonomy also outlawed slavery. Tensions escalated between the Anglo settlers and Mexican officials over slavery and land ownership until a new Mexican president, Antonio Lopez de Santa Ana, set the Mexican Constitution aside. The Texians rebelled and blood was shed at the Alamo and Goliad before an American victory at San Jacinto gained Texas independence in 1836.

Mexico never recognized Texas independence and the border was never clearly established. Culturally and religiously, the *Texians* were more closely aligned with the United States. As his last act as president, John Tyler had pushed through Congress a measure calling for annexation of Texas. Incoming President James K. Polk, who had campaigned on a platform of national expansion from sea to sea, moved quickly to admit Texas to statehood in 1845. With the Texas question settled, the eventual possession of California became a foregone conclusion and President Polk set his sights on achieving his larger prize. Editor and diplomat John L. Sullivan used the term "Manifest Destiny" in his publications, *The Democratic Review* and the *New York Morning News*, in 1845. After negotiating a treaty with Britain, establishing a border in the Oregon Territory, President Polk was now free to pursue California. After Mexico rebuffed U.S. negotiations to purchase California, Polk and the Manifest Destiny faction in Congress used a staged skirmish along the Mexican-U.S. border in Texas as an excuse for war. What the United States could not achieve diplomatically (though it still might have been possible) it would accomplish by force of arms. In May 1846, Congress officially declared war with its southern neighbor.

Events in California had been escalating quickly. Earlier that year, Fremont had led a troop of soldiers and mountain men back into California and bivouacked at Sutter's Fort. The Mexican *comandante* in the north, José Castro, ordered the Americans to leave California. Instead, Fremont proceeded to Monterey and met with U.S. Consul Thomas Larkin, who had been one of those secretly negotiating with the *Californios.*

Afraid of American incursion and internal insurrection, Castro confronted Fremont with armed troops. On a nearby peak in the Gabilan Mountains, Fremont raised the Stars and Stripes, made a brief show of resistance and then effected a strategic retreat into Oregon. He would not remain there long.

Historians disagree on whether Fremont next acted on his own initiative or whether he had received secret official orders from Washington D.C. to invade California. In June 1846, with Fremont's tacit support, a rowdy gaggle of American settlers in the northern California *pueblo* of Sonoma arrested General Mariano Vallejo, liberated his vast wine cellar, and loudly proclaimed the independent Bear Flag Republic of California. Fremont was hoping to force *Comandante* Castro's hand and draw him into conflict. Within weeks, Fremont assumed command of the Bear-Flaggers and merged them with his own troops, calling it the California Battalion. Fremont informed Sutter that California was now in American hands then raced to San Francisco Bay and, unopposed, spiked the Mexican guns mounted at the *Presidio.* (A decade earlier, General Vallejo had shifted the Mexican forces from the *Presidio* north to Sonoma, leaving the undefended bay garrison in the hands of a caretaker.) By this time, unconfirmed news of the war with Mexico had filtered into California and American warships under U.S. fleet Commodore John Drake Sloat had sailed into California ports. To protect Consul Larkin and other American interests, The *USS Portsmouth,* under Captain John B. Montgomery, had already entered the Port of Monterey without resistance on April 21st. But Sloat was cautious not to repeat Commodore Catesby-Jones's misstep without confirmation of war. Sloat questioned Fremont's actions and authority and hoped for a peaceful resolution of the conflict. However, by July, Sloat had been replaced by the younger, more aggressive Captain Robert F. Stockton, who embraced Fremont's actions and prepared for all-out war. The American flag was raised over Monterey and Captain Montgomery sailed into San Francisco Bay the following week, raising the Stars and Stripes up a makeshift pole in the sandy plaza in front of the Customs House, up from the muddy shoreline of Yerba Buena Cove on July 12, 1846. The United States was claiming California by right of conquest in war.

On the afternoon tide of July 31, 1846, the 445-ton ship *Brooklyn,* out of New York, left the choppy "Potato Patch" Pacific waters outside the Golden Gate, and entered the channel into San Francisco Bay, under full sail. A wind blew off the bay as the ship cautiously sailed past the quiet shadow of the undefended *Presidio* on the starboard side and the Marin headlands to port into calmer water as it rounded the shoreline curve into Yerba Buena Cove. After months of hard sailing from the east coast of America, around Cape Horn and across the Pacific to the Sandwich Islands before their ultimate destination of California, the hundreds of passengers felt relief. At long last, they had arrived at their new home.

Entering the cove, the excitement of arrival quickly turned to dismay. Most all the passengers were of the Mormon religion – The Church of Jesus Christ of Latter-Day Saints – and were refugees from religious persecution in the United States. Their leader and organizer of the long voyage was a young elder of the Church named Samuel Brannan. As they hugged the rail of the ship they were met with a familiar sight: the American flag flapping from the mast of the *USS*

Portsmouth at anchor in the cove. Gazing up, Brannan saw yet a second flag flying the stars and stripes from a pole on shore. These symbols represented the very nation his band of Saints, as they preferred to be known, were trying to flee. These Mormons had come to California to establish their own independent colony, to wrench it away from Mexico by force if necessary. And now the United States was in control of California as well. The Saints had arrived little more than a fortnight too late.

Notes

1. Max Arax, The Dreamt Land. Chasing Water and Dust Across California, New York: Vintage Books, 2019, p. 142.

2. Simon Winchester, Land, New York: Perennial, 2022, p. 138.

Chapter 4
Eastern Saint

"It is no small thing, in the blaze of this nineteenth century, to give men a new revelation, found a new religion, establish new forms of worship, to build a city with new laws, institutions, and orders of architecture, to establish ecclesiastic, civil and military jurisdiction, found colleges, send out missionaries and make proselytes in two hemispheres, yet all this has been done by Joe Smith, and that against every sort of opposition, ridicule and persecution."

– New York Sun
on the murder of Joseph Smith, 1844

"Mormonism, instead of exploding here [Nauvoo, Illinois] *as it was supposed it would, upon the death of the Prophet Joe Smith has continued as flourishing as ever."*

– New York Daily Tribune, April 30, 1845

At only 26 years, Samuel Brannan seemed young to be an elder of the Latter-Day Saints. However, his role in this emerging religion stemmed from his boyhood and his long relationship with the family, and the personage, of its founding Prophet, Joseph Smith.

The Mormon faith evolved at a time of tremendous religious fervor in the United States called the Second Great Awakening. Established Protestant denominations – the Anglicans, Lutherans, Congregationalists, Methodists, Baptists and Presbyterians – tried to maintain their flocks in the face of this evangelical Christianity proliferation, while any number of preachers, reformers, revivalists and faith healers roamed the countryside seeking converts to their unique brands of supernatural Christianity, all offering their particular spin on doctrine and dangling the certainty of heaven or hell in front of their congregations.

Growing up in a spiritually inclined upstate New York family during this confusion, the young farm boy, Joseph Smith, sought clarity about which religious path to follow. According to his testimony, he received a divine visitation instructing him that none of the existing churches held the authority of the true Christian faith and announcing his appointment as the Prophet who would establish Christ's renewed church on earth in these latter days. A few years later, Smith claimed he was directed to recover ancient sacred texts, which when translated from "reformed Egyptian", augmented the Christian Bible and formed the doctrinal basis of the Church of Jesus Christ of Latter-Day Saints, founded in 1830. His own publication of *The Book of Mormon* was a singular event in American literary history, although subsequent scholars and literary critics have puzzled over how to categorize the prodigious work. Among the early converts to this faith were Samuel Brannan's older sister, Mary Ann, and her husband, Alexander Badlam.

Samuel Brannan descended from Irish farm families in County Waterford. His father, Thomas (1755-1837/8), immigrated to America and made his home at Saco, Maine. His second wife was Sarah Knox Emery (1773-1837), allegedly the niece of Revolutionary War General Henry Knox, who had served as first Secretary of War under President Washington. Thomas and Sarah had six children, of which Samuel, born in 1819, was youngest.[1]

Leaving home, possibly to distance himself from an unhappy home life, the teenaged Brannan accompanied his sister to their new home in Plainesville Ohio, on the verge of civilization and close to the growing Mormon community at Kirtland. He received the blessing of the Church at the hand of Joseph Smith in 1835 designating priesthood authority. For a time, the Badlams either shared living accommodations with their Prophet neighbor or were frequent visitors and Samuel Brannan found himself deeply influenced by the association.

In person, Joseph Smith was a talented orator and persuasive preacher. But Smith instinctively recognized the need for broader communication to reach and instruct his rapidly growing flock of converts. Almost from the beginning, Joseph Smith authorized purchase of printing presses and type and the Church encouraged and supported establishment of newspapers in Mormon communities. The first of these church publications was *The Evening and the Morning Star,* published in Independence, Missouri in 1832 by William W. Phelps, until the press was destroyed a year later. It was succeeded by the *Messenger and Advocate* in 1834 in Kirtland, Ohio, edited by Oliver Cowdery. That paper was followed in Kirtland, in 1837, by the *Elder's Journal,* edited by Smith's brother, Don Carlos Smith. All these were monthly internal publications.

To learn a trade, and with Smith's encouragement, young Brannan became an apprentice printer, a position often – and ironically – called *printer's devil.* Acquiring the skills to put out a publication provided the clever Brannan with employability, while reaping the spiritual benefits of his earthly contribution to the Church. Brannan assisted in publication of the *Messenger and Advocate*. However, the American frontier was consumed by land speculation and Brannan's emerging entrepreneurism drew him into the frenzy. With borrowed money and a small inheritance, he made his first modest land deal, only to suffer loss with the nationwide depression and collapse of 1837. His acumen in property speculation would create and lose him fortunes over his lifetime.

Entering adulthood, Brannan yearned to see more of this expanding nation, now pushing up against the geographical barrier of the mighty Mississippi River. Brannan bought out the final year of his apprenticeship in 1839. He wandered through the newly settled states between the Alleghenies and the Mississippi, eventually arriving in New Orleans where his brother Thomas had settled. Together the siblings purchased a rebuilt printing press and launched a weekly literary publication. Sam was dazzled by the richness of cultures from Spain, France, the Caribbean, Africa and the American south. The exotic environment of creole society and the booming cotton trading economy of the Crescent City appealed to the hedonistic side of Brannan's nature, and likely conflicted with the more conservative values of his new-found religion. But the brutality of the slave-based economy appalled him, and he would remain staunchly abolitionist for the rest of his life. When Thomas died within days of being struck down by yellow fever, the publishing venture failed as well. Samuel abandoned the delta city and made his way back north up the Mississippi, picking up printing jobs along the way to pay his passage home.

Some evidence points to Brannan editing and publishing the anti-slavery *Gazette* in Indianapolis, Indiana, possibly using the same press he had purchased in New Orleans. Despite the failure of the paper, this stint in journalism imbedded in Brannan strong support of the ideals of Jacksonian Democracy.[2.] When the *Gazette* failed to turn a profit, Brannan abandoned his sojourn in the secular world and returned to his family in Ohio, renewing his religious faith and joining his brother-in-law Alexander Badlam in missionary work locally.

During this period Brannan appears to have met and married, or simply co-habited with a local woman named Hattie Hatch. Their union may have been religious only or possibly also civil, but in either case it proved contentious and unhappy. Unable to endure the acrimony of the relationship, Brannan sought solace with other women before finally walking away from the marriage. Although he would later remarry and have his desertion of his first wife approved by Joseph Smith, he seems not to have legally dissolved any prior marriage and the taint of bigamy would haunt Brannan for many years. Meanwhile, Badlam had moved his family from Ohio to Missouri, then on to Nauvoo, Illinois as anti-Mormon prejudice tuned violent at each new settlement. Brannan was recuperating from a bout with malaria at his sister's home in Nauvoo in 1844 when he was called for further missionary work, in the state of New York. The elders of the Church wanted a newspaper for converts in New York.

Sam Brannan returned to New York full of religious zeal but bereft of worldly goods. Nevertheless, the young missionary modeled his proselytizing after Joseph Smith, and soon caught the attention of Ann Eliza Corwin, daughter of a wealthy Mormon widow, Fanny Corwin of Connecticut. With her mother's approval, "Lizzie" and Sam were married and he enjoyed a degree of financial security while he helped George Leach and William Smith (another of the Prophet's brothers) edit the new paper. The first edition of *The Prophet* came off the press May 1844. The following year it would evolve into the *New York Messenger,* with Brannan as editor-in-chief.

New York journalism enjoyed a vibrancy dating back to colonial times. The earliest newspaper in the colony had been the *New York Gazette* in 1725. *The New York Journal* had been at the center of the landmark libel trial of publisher John Peter Zenger in 1735, which established the primacy of freedom of the press. By the 1840s there were hundreds of publications in New York. Washington Irving, Walt Whitman and Herman Melville were among the literary giants whose early work appeared in the New York press. In the spirit of Jacksonian Democracy, the so-called penny press papers such as the *New York Sun,* made both mass circulation and profitability a reality. Every commercial sector, special interest, political, religious or fraternal organization had their distinct publication. *The Prophet* was founded in part to support the campaign of Joseph Smith for the presidency in 1844. It resembled other Mormon newspapers and reprinted pieces from them. Correspondence from the faithful helped fill the pages of small, gray type. Among the news items was the busy schedule of speaking engagements throughout New York by Elder Samuel Brannan.

Meanwhile, anti-Mormon prejudice continued to escalate. Successful missionary evangelism had swelled the Nauvoo population to approaching 10,000. Suspicion among non-Mormons that Smith put his church above the law, combined with fear of Mormon block voting compounded existing friction over distinct church practices bringing events near to crisis. Tipping the scales against the new faith appears to have been rumors of the practice of spiritual wifery, or plural marriage. In fact, Joseph Smith claimed to have been instructed to implement such practice, and he, himself, is reported to have had as many as 30 spiritual wives, but the practice was held confidential among the Saints leadership. As word leaked out, it became more than the surrounding populations could tolerate. In June 1844, Joseph Smith and his elder brother Hyrum were pulled from a jail cell in Carthage, Illinois and killed by an angry mob. Sam Brannan laid out the front page of *The Prophet* with a broad black border surrounding the story of Smith's martyrdom on July 20.

Because both Smith brothers had been killed, there was no apparent successor to the Prophet. A political power struggle for leadership ensued. In the end, a bull-necked, strong-willed acolyte named Brigham Young emerged. Lacking Smith's charisma, but possessing strong organizational skills, Brigham Young determined that for their safety and survival, his Mormon followers must leave the United States and establish a homeland of their own in the American Far West. That decision, in many ways, altered and intertwined the destiny of a man called Sam Brannan and a land called California.

Brigham Young determined that the exodus of his people should be accomplished in three phases. He, himself, would lead a vanguard party of Mormons overland, across the North American prairies and Rocky Mountains, to search for a suitable location in the west to build their new Zion. Once a site was selected, the remaining Saints would follow and join them. Young never publicly confirmed his intended destination, preferring to keep his options open and his ultimate goal confidential. While never totally ruling California out, it becomes clear from his various correspondence that the Pacific coast would never have been his destination of choice.

With the advent of hostilities with Mexico, the so-called "Mormon problem" in Missouri and Illinois became an annoying irritant to the federal government in Washington D.C., otherwise about to engage in a foreign war. Still, the thought of many armed Mormon militia, roaming through unguarded U.S. territory, much less invading foreign (Mexican) soil could be seen as treasonous. And an independent Mormon colony in the west could block U.S. westward expansion. President James K. Polk sought to use the Mormons to the country's advantage, without antagonizing the religion's enemies. On the eve of war with Mexico, in a political balancing act, to co-opt Latter-Day Saints loyalty, as well as to augment federal troop strength, Polk negotiated with Young to form a separate unit of Mormon volunteer soldiers, the only such religious unit in U.S. military history. Young saw this arrangement as a good-will means to ensure a degree of federal protection for his emigrating followers, while enabling many Mormons to be taken west at federal expense, with their military salaries providing a much-needed source of hard cash. More than 500 nominally patriotic young Mormon men volunteered with their leader's blessing to form the Mormon Battalion. Ill-equipped and poorly trained, the "battalion boys" served uncomfortably with regular troops from Missouri and made the long trek from Fort Leavenworth down the Santa Fe Trail. Once New Mexico Territory had been secured against any Mexican counter-offensive and the region pacified against hostile Native Americans, the battalion, under overall command of General Stephen Kearny, would march west across the Arizona desert into southern California. There they would reinforce U.S. forces securing California and would be discharged at the end of the war.

Young's plan called for these Mormon veterans to join with others of their faith who would have arrived in California by sea. Young's third prong of emigration called for shiploads of Saints to evacuate the United States and make the long voyage around South America to California. There, these refugees would establish a foothold on the Pacific coast and form the nucleus of a future Latter-Day community – and if appropriate possibly an alternate Zion. To organize and lead such an effort on the east coast, Brigham Young turned to the head of the Mormon movement in New York, Samuel Brannan.

Brannan was not a unanimous choice for this leadership role. The young publisher was already proving controversial. Despite his tremendous enthusiasm in preaching sermons throughout the state and facilitating travel of Mormon converts to the Church's center in Nauvoo, Brannan had otherwise run afoul of the Church. Together with the Prophet's brother, William Smith, Brannan had been officiating at plural marriages without authorization and had himself been sealed in a celestial marriage – polygamy still a guarded secret and extended only to the highest leadership of the Church. In addition, Brannan's various business enterprises were raising eyebrows among church officials. Finally, his close political connections to the Democratic Party and support of the Polk campaign for president had resulted in substantial patronage for the publisher of *The Prophet* but possibly compromised his total allegiance to the Church. Brannan was "disfellowshipped and cut off" from the church in 1845. However, after appeals by William Smith and Elder Parley P. Pratt on his behalf, and Brannan's own travel to Nauvoo for a hearing on his excommunication where he promised repentance, the apostles of the Church (all polygamists themselves) followed Brigham Young's counsel to "throw a mantle over it all" and reinstated Brannan soon after. At this point, Brannan swung his allegiance from William Smith and fully subscribed to the leadership of Brigham Young.

U.S. Government involvement in the resettlement of the Mormons involved much more intrigue. Wherever their hegira took them, their presence was likely to interfere with U.S. foreign policy and negotiations with Britain over Oregon or with Mexico over California. By 1841, William G. Tae had established a trading post of the British Hudson's Bay Company within the cove at Yerba Buena, fueling speculation about British intentions in northern California. However, a large contingent of loyal Americans successfully relocated to California could only bolster President Polk's aim of securing California. Through his political connections, Samuel Brannan became caught up in a scheme traced to former U.S. Postmaster General Amos Kendall, a close advisor to both former president Andrew Jackson and President Polk, to guarantee the safe passage of the Mormon parties in return for territorial rights to half of any newly occupied Mormon lands in the west. Brannan agreed but was overruled by a suspicious Brigham Young, anxious to be independent of the United States.[3] Perhaps Brannan had cleverly engineered a deception, securing much needed financing from the government speculators, while knowing all along that Brigham Young would never sign-off on the deal.

In September 1845, Brigham Young expressed his desire for Brannan, his "press paper" and "ten thousand of his bretheren" to be settled on the shores of San Francisco Bay.[4.] Eastern Saints who may have been considering relocating to Nauvoo or even migrating overland to the west, now read an admonition in the *Messenger*

> *"to make our journey to the place of our future destiny by water, as soon as arrangements can be conveniently made."*[5]

The paper continued:

> *"Saints in the eastern states can emigrate to the other side of the Rocky Mountains by water, with half the expense attending a journey by land, and they can take many things that could not be taken over the mountains."*[6]

The next edition offered the incentive of reduced fare if sufficient passengers could be recruited to charter a ship. The articles, penned by Elder Orson Pratt, urged haste to take advantage of the summer season in the southern hemisphere and fully endorsed Elder Samuel Brannan as leader of the expedition.

Sam Brannan faced a daunting challenge, one that would test his faith, require all his skills and consume all his limited resources. He was personally in debt. His urbane wife Lizzie held serious reservations about leaving civilization for unknown distant shores, though her devout mother, Mother Corwin, fully accepted the Church's call to emigrate and follow the direction of her son-in-law. (In addition, Lizzie Brannan was about to give birth to their first child, Samuel Jr.) While the Church of the Saints aspired to salvation in a celestial paradise, its daily operation was firmly grounded in the material world. Church businesses were operated at a profit; land and other investments generally generated a healthy return, and the Church extracted a voluntary tithe from its members, creating a substantial operating fund. In addition to a fare of 50 dollars per adult passenger and 25 dollars for children, Brannan also sought to offset his costs by securing a government contract to carry naval freight onboard, although this effort failed. Thus, while Brannan prayed for guidance and spent the fall of 1845 recruiting followers, sufficient Church funding found its way to help him charter a ship and supply it adequately for a six-month voyage and beyond. In mid-December, an extra edition of the *New York Messenger* announced that the ship *Brooklyn* had been chartered and the services of Captain Abel W. Richardson, a non-Mormon but an experienced mariner of fine moral character, had been secured and a sailing date had been set for one month hence.[7]

January 1846 was a frenzied period for the Eastern Saints as they surreptitiously drifted into New York City, trying not to call attention to the upcoming departure. In between preaching and recruiting passengers, Brannan hurried back and forth between the city and Washington D.C., still trying to secure federal financial assistance. In the process his political connections alerted him to possible government intervention, fearing the Mormon militia might ally themselves with a foreign power against the United States. Given their history, Mormons had no reservoir of allegiance to the U.S. (in England, some 15,000 souls had converted to Mormonism, and a third of them, possibly still loyal to Britain, had already migrated to the United States) If the government was prepared to intercept Brigham Young's land party with force, it would possibly search the *Brooklyn* for carrying arms as well (The *Brooklyn* would, in fact, carry a supply of muskets and small arms for possible use in securing a beachhead in California, and would acquire a number of rifles and cannon enroute in the Sandwich Islands). Brannan passed this warning on to Brigham Young, who believed that President Polk conspired with state and local militias to exterminate the Mormon Church. Young accelerated his own timetable to begin his journey west.

On February 4, 1846, Brigham Young led the first wagons across the Mississippi River in search of a new homeland. That same afternoon, The *Brooklyn* slipped from its moorings in New York harbor, flying a pennant saying "*Oregon,*" to disguise its destination. On board were about 240 Mormon men, women and children (the precise number is unclear) as well as the crew and a small contingent of gentiles (non-believers). In the hold, in addition to all the passenger baggage, were stored the requisite tools, machinery and agricultural supplies to establish a colony, including three grist mills and Sam Brannan's disassembled iron Acorn printing press, along with boxes of six, eight and ten-point metal type slugs used at the *New York Messenger* and a quantity of newsprint paper. Carefully wrapped and stowed in Brannan's own luggage, the type held firmly in place in its matrix, the typography already pre-selected, was the masthead of Brannan's intended new newspaper: *The California Star.*

Notes

1. "The Brannan Family" *Saunders Family History*, Chapter 9, revised Jan. 2021, pp. 66-78 http://www.saundersfamilyhistory.com>images, retrieved Feb. 3, 2023.

2. Jacksonian Democracy was a 19th century political philosophy brought about by the election of President Andrew Jackson. It advocated greater rights for the common man and more citizen participation in government. It called for universal [white] male suffrage without property requirements and national expansion under the banner of Manifest Destiny. The issue of slavery was carefully avoided.

3. W. Ray Luce, "The Mormon Battalion: A Historical Accident?" *Utah Historical Quarterly*, vol. 42, no. 1, 1974, https://ISSUU.com>uhq>volume42_1974_number 1.

4. Letter from Brigham Young to Samuel Brannan, Sept. 15, 1845, Brigham Young Collection, LDS Archives.

5. *New York Messenger,* Nov. 15, 1845.

6. Ibid.

7. Ibid, December 13, 1845.

William Briggs

Chapter 5
Brooklyn's *Pilgrims*

"The influence which their [Latter-Day Saints] *arrival and settlement must have upon the present condition of California, is quite uncertain; but should the tide of emigration continue to flow in (as it undoubtedly will) California must very soon become a very different country from what it has been – civilly, socially, morally and religiously."*

– Samuel C. Damon,
The Friend (Honolulu), July 1, 1846

"We had a truly prosperous voyage, as we were promised before leaving New York."

– John M. Horner,
Brooklyn passenger,
"Voyage of the Ship Brooklyn," 1906

The faithful prayed for deliverance. Only days out from New York, the *Brooklyn* sailed into a violent Atlantic winter storm. Waves tossed the ship about like a cork. Mountains of angry black-green water hurled themselves at the hardwood hull of the *Brooklyn*. On the other side of that hull, the ship's company huddled beneath battened hatches. Frightened children wailed. Women tied themselves into their bunks. Stomachs dry-retched into wooden pails and bodies collided, unable to stand, as the motion pitched, and furniture and cargo shifted. These passengers had left behind relatives, jobs, homes and all familiar. They had abandoned the land where their Puritan ancestors had also sought religious refuge, and they had renounced the country their forefathers had fought for in the Revolution. All to follow young Sam Brannan to a new promised land, these modern-day Israelites, these Latter-Day Saints. Even Captain Richardson, having lashed the wheel and joined the passengers below deck, acknowledged that they were now in God's hands.

To accommodate Brannan's flock, carpenters had constructed partitioned cubicles along both sides of the passenger deck, providing at least a modicum of privacy for each family, but with more than 200 individuals, the space was cramped. A single table ran the length of the deck between the compartments. There the Saints took their communal meals, children received lessons, people read, sang hymns or attended religious services, seated on hard wooden benches, bolted to the floor. A large library accompanied the Saints for reading, schooling the children and establishing a school in California. Brannan would later claim to have paid for the refitting at his own expense.

With almost military-like organization, Brannan laid out a schedule of rules and responsibilities for his people, regarding meal preparation, cleanliness and social behavior in such confined space. With little objection, the congregation conformed to the daily routine and settled in for the long voyage. Brannan also produced an agreement, signed by the male Saints, that the entire company would work collaboratively to retire the ship's debt and the fruit of their labor would be held in trust for three years by "S. Brannan & Co." to prepare the way for the advent of the main Mormon party and provide for the communal good. While not as significant as the historic *Mayflower Compact,* signed by the earlier religious pilgrims, this agreement bound the Saints to each other, and their assets to Samuel Brannan should the agreement be breeched. Brannan's heavy-handed, acquisitive leadership bred resentment for years to come.

In the cargo hold, in addition to Brannan's press and a large inventory of farm implements and hardware of all sorts, the ship sailed with a pair of dairy cows, two score swine and several crates of fowl. While not the two-by-two of all species on Noah's ark, the *Brooklyn* carried the nucleus of a permanent agricultural community to be established at their destination. Like Brigham Young, Samuel Brannan was somewhat circumspect about this final destination. Most of the Saints believed they were to establish their own colony in California and that the overland party of Mormons would eventually join them there. Such were Brannan's intentions as well, but knowing neither what reception to expect in Mexican-held California nor what President Young's disposition on California would finally be, Brannan also considered Oregon or Vancouver Island as possible destinations. Time would tell.

After several days, the tempest abated, and the *Brooklyn* sailed into calmer seas. However, the gale had blown the craft far to the east, nearing the Cape Verde Islands off the coast of Africa. In one of several serendipitous happenings on the voyage, this allowed Captain Richardson to pick up the northeast trade winds and skirt the "nose" of Brazil, that eastern-most point of South America, once tucked into the African landmass in the days of the single Gondwanaland southern supercontinent. Catching the trades allowed the

Brooklyn to make up some time lost during the storm, as Captain Richardson was anxious to navigate Cape Horn before the winter ice formed. The three-masted, square-rigged[1] *Brooklyn* was already eleven years old and showed her age. She was built for transport, not speed. As a passenger ship, she was more of a plow horse than a thoroughbred. But for Brannan, she had been affordable and available as most other ships sought lucrative government contracts in anticipation of war with Mexico.

Once across the equator in early March, the *Brooklyn* floated becalmed in the doldrums of the South Atlantic. The oppressive tropical heat beat down on the motionless ship, further casting a pall over the voyage. Death had stowed away on the *Brooklyn*. Nine of their number, including several children, had died during the storm and its aftermath, claimed by diarrhea, consumption or scarlet fever. The Saints comforted the grieving parents as best they could as the weighted shrouds slid into everlasting rest at sea. One child buried at sea was the one-year-old son of Charles Burr. Yet the entire ship's company rejoiced when the Burr family was blessed with the birth onboard of another son. They named him John Atlantic Burr. A crewman also succumbed to a stomach illness and a two more Saints would perish later in the voyage.

More than half a century later, James Skinner recalled the voyage he had made as a child, including being becalmed at sea:

> *"The seas were like molten glass...It was so hot*
> *that the pitch was drawn out of the ship's seams,*
> *Oh, how the people suffered."*[2]

Catching a strong wind, the *Brooklyn* sailed through temperate waters of the South Atlantic and made for Cape Horn by early April. Captain Richardson sailed far south to the 60th parallel to get a push around the Cape, avoiding Tierra del Fuego, and heading into the treacherous Straits of Magellan, feared by mariners from the time of Francis Drake. Captain and crew were well-aware of the dangers posed by the ice clogged waters of two colliding oceans. The temperatures plummeted to freezing; all hands were required to hack the vessel free of sea ice. Stowed in most every sailor's sea bag was a worn copy of Richard Henry Dana's book, *Two Years Before the Mast*, published in 1840, with detailed description of frozen sails and rigging, ice-bound hulls and looming icebergs in the waters at the tip of South America. The efforts of all able-bodied aboard kept the ship free of ice and she sailed into better weather and moderate seas, passing into the Pacific Ocean without further incident.

Charting a northward course along the Chilean coast of South America, *the Brooklyn's* store of firewood had been almost exhausted by the cold of the passage around the Horn and the demands of cooking for hundreds of people. Likewise, the inventory of drinking water had become depleted and what remained had become foul with algae. Captain Richardson sailed for Valparaiso, Chile to resupply, but fierce weather caused a changed course and the *Brooklyn* headed instead for the Juan Fernandez Islands.

The Juan Fernandez Islands are an archipelago of three main volcanic islands set in the Pacific some 400 miles west of the Chilean mainland. Originally discovered in 1574 by Juan Fernandez, a Spanish sailor seeking to avoid the northerly

Humboldt current, the islands provided fresh water, food and fuel as well as sanctuary for 17th and 18th century pirates preying on Spanish shipping between Peru and Chile. The islands were home to the Scottish castaway Alexander Selkirk who spent four years alone there. His story would have been familiar to the voyagers on the *Brooklyn*; Selkirk had been the inspiration for the wildly popular novel *Robinson Crusoe*.[3] By the 19th century the island had been used as a Chilean penal colony as well as a station for fur seal trappers and British and American whalers, as described by Dana in *Two Years Before the Mast*. By the time of the Saints' visit, the Juan Fernandez Islands were largely uninhabited. The few islanders would be the first human contact, on the first dry land, the *Brooklyn* had encountered since leaving New York.

Once again, Captain Richardson's navigation was spot-on. The *Brooklyn* anchored safely away from the pounding surf and westerly Pacific winds in a calm inlet in the lee of Alejandro Selkirk Island, the largest in the group, The travelers rowed ashore in the small dinghy and were met by a couple friendly families of *mestizos* (mixed race inhabitants) who greeted them with pidgin Spanish and hand gestures. The first order of business was a funeral. Weeks earlier, one of the Saints, a pregnant mother of seven, had suffered a fall from a ladder in high seas and was confined to her bunk with serious injury. Sensing her final days, Laura Goodwin begged to be buried on land rather than at sea. As the *Brooklyn* rounded Cape Horn and sailed into the Pacific, Laura had succumbed to her injuries. The party of pilgrims broke out shovels from their supply in the hold and carried out her wish in a cave on Alejandro Selkirk Island. The gloom of this death would be offset in the coming weeks by the birth of another baby. Dr. and Mrs. John Robbins, who had already lost two sons during the Atlantic crossing now had a daughter. They called her Georgiana, her middle name Pacific.

Once ashore, the Saints stretched their sea-legs on solid ground. They offered prayers of thanksgiving and then set about replenishing their supplies. Firewood was bundled. Casks were cleaned and refilled with some 18,000 gallons of fresh water.[4] The company was overjoyed to find fresh fruit and some vegetables available from the locals to fight recurring bouts of scurvy. And while there was no native fauna on the islands, there were feral goats and pigs brought by previous occupants, as well as an abundance of fish and shellfish. The Saints ate heartily and salted enough food for the next leg of the voyage at very low cost. Once again, fortune had followed the Saints.

One of the voyagers, William Glover, recalled:

"It would have cost hundreds of dollars [in Valparaiso]*; thus showing to us the hand of the Lord."*[5]

As an afterthought, they also gave thanks to their captain.

After a week, the restocked *Brooklyn* set course for the Sandwich Islands (Hawai'i) and, despite a period of calm in equatorial waters, arrived at the port of Honolulu six weeks later, on June 20, 1846.

Despite his arrogant demeanor and often secretive behavior, Samuel Brannan commanded and received respect

William Briggs

and obedience to his authority. However, before arrival in Hawai'i, the social order cracked temporarily.

Young Mormon women, according to non-Mormon passenger Edward Kemble,

> *"were modest and discreet, and probably no emigrant ship ever crossed an ocean – certainly none ever sailed to California – whose female passengers at the end of a long voyage preserved their reputations as unspotted as those of the Brooklyn."*[6]

However, one female passenger, an attractive widow named Lucy Eagar, sought and encouraged attention among the men on board. She may have made overtures to Brannan, himself, only to be rebuffed. One man talked of making Lucy his second wife. Polygamy was an open secret in the Mormon community, but public acknowledgement was forbidden. Brannan reacted strongly, accusing members of spreading false doctrine and acting "with wicked and licentious conduct,"[7] thereby avoiding mention of plural marriage. In his official capacity as leader, Brannan excommunicated three men and Lucy Eagar. Many of the ship's company thought Brannan had abused his authority. Months later, in California, Brannan was sued in court by those he had accused but was exonerated.

The Hawaiian Island chain of volcanic mountain tops became inhabited by intrepid Polynesian sailors as long as a thousand years ago. These early Hawaiians developed a unique culture and remained largely isolated from the rest of the world for centuries. They were "discovered" in the late 18th century by the great British explorer Captain James Cook who named

68

them for his patron, the Earl of Sandwich. With British backing, King Kamehameha I unified the islands into a kingdom in the first decades of the 19th century. From that point, the islands became heavily involved in Pacific trade and were a regular port of call on the trade route between Asia and North America. Soon religious missionaries from several countries followed the whalers and merchant mariners to Hawai'i, proselytizing and converting the local population. To help finance their journey, the Mormons had brought a large quantity of Bibles onboard the *Brooklyn* for other Christian missionaries in the islands.

Skirting the extinct Diamond Head crater, the *Brooklyn* anchored in the roads outside Honolulu Harbor. Nearby bobbed the American naval frigate, *USS Congress.* Presently, Commodore Robert Stockton transferred to the *Brooklyn* to interview Captain Richardson. As leader of the contingent, Brannan joined the conversation and learned for the first time that a state of war existed between the United States and Mexico. Wary that Stockton may try to impound the cargo of firearms on board the *Brooklyn*, Brannan was relieved when Stockton instead recruited the Mormons to attack Mexican defenses at Yerba Buena and helped Brannan acquire some 150 vintage rifles for the pending assault. Stockton probably saw these American civilians as expendable shock troops to occupy the Mexicans at San Francisco Bay and claim it for the United States, while he, himself, led an invasion of the Alta California capital of Monterey. On the voyage between Hawai'i and California, Samuel Ladd, a military veteran in the Mormon company, drilled the young men in close order marching on deck and firearm familiarity. In the end, neither Yerba Buena nor Monterey would be actively defended by Mexican troops and the Saints would not be enlisted as Christian soldiers for the United States.

In Honolulu, Sam Brannan gave a lengthy interview to the local newspaper, *The Polynesian*, which reported the visit of the Mormons to Hawai'i:

> *"They have on board about $30,000, invested in agricultural implements and the necessary articles for forming a settlement, with a stock of clothing for two years. The men are said to be supplied with rifles and know how to use them. Tents have been provided for habitations until houses can be erected. Their destination is the north side of the bay of San Francisco, where they design to establish a commercial town."*[8]

The article continued:

> *"Capt. Richardson speaks in the highest terms of the correct deportment and general harmony of his numerous passengers in every respect. Religious services and a school have been regularly held. They are well supplied with schoolbooks. Mr. Brannan has with him a press and intends establishing a paper to be called the California Star."*[9]

Hawai'i apparently found these Mormons quite newsworthy, and Brannan eagerly promoted their cause to the press. Another newspaper, *The Friend*, devoted six columns to discussing the religion and the intentions of his followers. Brannan told *The Friend* that California had been chosen as the new Zion and that their brethren crossing the plains at that time would rendezvous and settle along San Francisco Bay.[10] This announcement was premature and ultimately wrong.

Sweet floral fragrances wafted on cooling trade winds as the Saints enjoyed an extended week in Honolulu. They interacted with other Christian groups, completed laundry and housekeeping chores, refreshed themselves and once again resupplied the *Brooklyn*. A few Saints, too ill to travel on, remained in Hawai'i; one would be the 11th and last of the company to die enroute. News from Commodore Stockton and Brannan's own initiative cast the die for California instead of Oregon or Vancouver Island. North of the Sandwich Islands, the North Pacific current flows clockwise toward the coast of North America. Except for a few windless days again, the current pushed the *Brooklyn* to California in a month's time and the Saints sailed into San Francisco Bay on July 31st. The *Brooklyn* rounded the shoreline and anchored in deep water outside the small cove. They had traveled nearly 24,000 land miles in five months: stopping but twice, likely the longest religious pilgrimage in history.

The dissonance at seeing the United States flag flying over Yerba Buena Cove was palatable. Apocryphal stories recalled Brannan muttering something like, *"There's that damned flag."* Some angry Saints called for turning around and sailing to Oregon. A detachment of sailors and marines from the *USS Portsmouth* rowed to the *Brooklyn*, delighted to see so many well-groomed women onboard. With great courtesy, the officer in charge confirmed the facts by welcoming the passengers to the United States. The open gun ports on the

American war sloop easily dissuaded any thought of challenging the American navy.

In his own luggage, Sam Brannan had brought a folded flag of his own, designed by Church leaders and sent with the sea-borne Saints. The white silk ensign featured an image of the Virgin, surrounded by a dozen stars, representing the biblical and Latter-Day twelve apostles. Intended to represent and fly over a new theocracy in the West, The Kingdom of God, the banner posed a threat to United States' sovereignty and could once again unleash the furies that had driven the Mormons from Missouri and Illinois. Brannan wisely kept the flag under wraps.[11] If California was indeed now in the hands of the United States, he would pivot and exploit the new relationship to the benefit of his Church – and his own personal ambition. He had arrived in California and there he would stay.

Notes

1. Square-rigged: Sails and rigging perpendicular to the line of the ship.

2. James Skinner, *Autobiography*, LDS Archives, MS 6587.

3. Written by Daniel Defoe and published in 1719 as a fictionalized autobiography of a marooned sailor, the complete title was The life and Strange Surprizing Adventure of Robinson Crusoe, of York, Mariner: who lived Eight and Twenty Years all alone in an un-inhabited island on the coast of America near the mouth of the Great River of Oroonoque; Having been cast on shore by shipwreck, wherein all the Men perished but himself. With an account how he was at last as strangely delivered by Pyrates. Written by Himself.

4. "Progress of the Mormon Emigrants from this City," *New York Daily Tribune*, August 27, 1846.

5. William Glover, The Mormons in California, Los Angeles: Glen Dawson, 1954, p. 16.

6. Edward Cleveland Kemble, A Kemble Reader: Stories of California, 1846-1848, Fred Blackburn Rogers ed., San Francisco Historical Society, 1963, p. 17.

7. *Millennial Star* 9, no. 20, October 15, 1847.

8. "Arrival of the Brooklyn with Emigrants for California," *The Polynesian,* June 27, 1846, pp. 22-23.

9. Ibid.

10. *The Friend*, July 1, 1846, p. 101.

11. Decades later, Brannan would display the flag as a souvenir of his journey. It was stolen about 1870 and never seen again.

Chapter 6
Brannan's Star

"The STAR will be an independent paper uninfluenced by those in power or the fear of the abuse of power, or of patronage or favor."

– Samuel Brannan,
The California Star, January 16, 1847

"San Francisco bay being the safest and most commodious harbor on the entire coast of the Pacific, some point on it must be the great mart of the western world. We believe Yerba Buena is the point."

– E.P. Jones,
The California Star, January 30, 1847

The moment the Saints disembarked onto dry land, Yerba Buena became a Mormon town. The Saints nearly tripled the hamlet's population. Once Captain John B. Montgomery of the *USS Portsmouth*, military commander in Yerba Buena, granted the Saints permission to land, the passengers unloaded their baggage and livestock from their "Noah's ark" onto the small sandy beach, where the high tide lapped the foot of Clay Street. No sooner had they erected their tents around the cove, surrounded by wind-flattened mesquite and manzanita which sheltered coyotes and other wildlife, than they industriously began building a community. Not only did the presence of women and children have a civilizing effect on the rough camp, but also the diverse skills and trades brought by these pilgrims were quickly employed. Many found shelter in the old adobe Casa Grande. Others sheltered from the wind in the Customs House. A small group made their home in the cloisters of old Mission Dolores, about four miles away. Tents were soon replaced by make-shift wooden shelters, in turn converted into low adobe buildings. The families spread across the breadth of the peninsula, seeking work at the *ranchos* and interacting with the *Californios.* Several women found employment at the new Portsmouth House Hotel. Menfolk found work in lumber camps, planting wheatfields or constructing dwellings. All the income was pooled by Sam Brannan for common use. Some Mormons, chaffing at the heavy-handed administration of S. Brannan & Co., sought to distance themselves from their appointed leader, but most of the Saints remained steadfastly loyal to Sam Brannan and formed a remarkably cohesive community. Certainly, many of them believed they were the advance party laying the foundation for a New Jerusalem, as soon as the thousands of other Latter-Day Saint faithful would make their way to California.

Edward Kemble, the young printer's devil apprentice who had accompanied his patron, Sam Brannan, on board the *Brooklyn*, and who would go on to play an important leading role in our story, years later recalled those first days in Yerba Buena in an article in the *Sacramento Daily Union:*

> *"The town proper of those nursing days was cuddled in the lap of that broad slope of hard native earth extending down from Dupont street to the beach thirty yards below Montgomery street*

*and bounded north and south by the two ravines
that came down from the hills about on lines of
Jackson and California streets. Between these
gullies, therefore, behold the town proper of Yerba
Buena. The half-breed babe – the half Mexican and
half 'foreign' prodigy, whose infant lineaments are
scarcely recognizable in the stately San Francisco.
Outside of these limits it was all 'suburban' –
pastoral – wild."*[1]

Once convinced the new arrivals presented little
subversive threat, Captain Montgomery worked to integrate
them into the commercial and social life of the village,
maintaining the Mormons as an additional wedge against
possible Mexican resistance to the American take-over of Alta
California. Several of the men were formed into a home guard
to protect against any Mexican attacks – which never came.
Whether by pragmatism, residual patriotism or resignation,
most of the Saints worked through their resentment and anger
toward the United States and moved on with their new lives.

Edward Kemble further recalled those first days in
California:

*"After seeing their wives and goods safely
bestowed...the emigrants proceeded to form a
Labor and Trading Association, of which Brannan
was President...contracts for labor and for the sale
of such of such articles as were to be manufactured
by the company were made, and parties dispatched
into the country or out upon the bay, in different
capacities as woodmen, launchmen, dairymen,
millers etc. A settlement* [to be called New Hope]

was established on the Stanislaus [River]. *to which
a number of families were removed."*[2]

In order to repay the remaining debt from the passage, S. Brannan & Co. contracted to supply the *Brooklyn* with a shipload of redwood timber, which the old ship took on board and slipped out of San Francisco Bay in September, bound for Monterey, the Sandwich Islands and eventually the trading ports of China, where the lumber would fetch a healthy profit. This debt reduction protected the cash flow of the Saints' communal funds and provided Brannan greater flexibility in administering and investing the accounts, which he treated as his own personal purse.

No sooner had Brannan off-loaded his printing press than he moved to put it to use. With the help of several strong men, Brannan installed his five-ton press on the second floor of Nathan Spear's mule-powered grist mill on yet-unnamed Clay Street, between Montgomery and Kearny Streets. Shortly thereafter, the press was relocated to a new adobe construction adjoining Brannan's house behind the Custom House at the plaza, now Portsmouth Square. As he readied his equipment to produce a newspaper, he made a significant – and perhaps personal – decision. Rather than publish a paper exclusively for and about his Latter-Day Saint followers, as he had done in New York, Brannan would cover this wider new world and provide news of interest to the entire community. Greater readership should yield greater profitability. While no less a devout Mormon, Brannan was inching away from the clannish insularity imposed by the Church and sensing the attraction of the secular world. In time, this divide would prove too great to straddle.

Within a month of United States occupation of Yerba Buena, Captain Montgomery appointed his second in command, Lieutenant Washington A. Bartlett, as *alcalde* (mayor) of the sleepy village by the bay. Although the relationship between Brannan and Bartlett would often be contentious – Brannan assumed significant temporal as well as spiritual authority over the Mormon population – Brannan's press benefitted from a contract to publish governmental notices. Among the earliest announcements published were *Rules and Regulations for the Trade of the Bay,* anti-fraud regulations for the tallow trade, deeds, programs and an announcement for a reception for Governor Stockton in October. But Brannan carefully avoided his paper becoming a governmental organ and took public issue with governmental wartime censorship restrictions and other municipal regulations administered under martial law.

The California Star would not become California's first newspaper. (Years later, editor and California newspaper historian Edward Kemble would somewhat facetiously claim that Brannan at least conceived *the idea* of a newspaper first.) The distinction of being first goes instead to *The Californian,* first published on August 15, 1846, in Monterey, by frontier dentist Robert B. Semple and Walter Colton, naval chaplain from the *USS Congress,* who became *alcalde* and judge in Monterey. Both men had some prior newspaper printing experience. The new publishing firm was designated Colton & Semple.

An old printing press, built in Boston, had been used for book printing and Mexican government proclamations by Agustin V. Zamorano, secretary to Mexican Governor Echeandia, in the 1830s. Thus, Zamorano had become the first printer in California. The equipment suffered from wear and poor maintenance and Zamorano's enterprise faltered. The press itself was brought to Sonoma by Northern Military Department General Mariano Vallejo for a time and then returned to the old capital of Alta California, where it was found in the Monterey Custom House at the time of the American invasion and repurposed for an English language newspaper.

The Californian's first edition carried very old news about Congress declaring war with Mexico as well as poems, gossip and scraps of news. It also made note of the arrival of *"La Frigata Brooklyn"* with a group of Mormon emigrants to Yerba Buena. The paper was bi-lingual, with English on one side and Spanish printed on the other side of the recycled cigarette paper used as newsprint. The page size was slightly larger than letter size and allowed only two columns. Stories were not separated by rules or leading (spacing). The typefaces were badly worn, some letters were missing, and the inking was uneven. The annual subscription rate was five dollars. At the time the non-Native American population of Alta California was estimated at not more than about 9,000 *Californios* and perhaps another thousand non-Hispanic foreigners.

Notably, *The Californian* editorialized for development of a mail service in California and called for a constitutional convention to petition official territorial annexation by the United States government. Among the governing principles published in the first edition *of The Californian* were the following:

> *"This is the first paper ever published in California, and though issued upon a small sheet,*

is intended it shall contain matter that will be read with interest...we shall maintain. An entire and utter severance of all political connexion [sic] with Mexico, we renounce at once and forever all fealty to her laws, all obedience to her mandates...We shall maintain freedom of speech and the press, and those great principles of religious toleration, which allows every man to worship God according to the dictates of his own conscience...We shall go for California—for all her interests, social, civil and religious—encouraging every thing that promotes these, resisting every thing that can do them harm."[3]

Colton and Semple continued weekly co-editorship of *The Californian* until April 1847, when Colton resigned for health and other job commitments. Although absent much of the time pursuing real estate ventures near Sonoma, Semple continued editing the paper in Monterey for another month before deciding the Monterey market was too limited and packing up and moving his enterprise to an adobe house augmented by a windmill in Yerba Buena, where it first competed and would ultimately merge with *The California Star.*

By October 1846, Sam Brannan had published *An Extra in Advance of The CALIFORNIA STAR,* a half-sheet published front and back, featuring news of General Zachary Taylor's campaign in Mexico. This preview edition of the *California Star* sold for one *real* (12 and one-half cents U.S.). Under the masthead listing S. Brannan as "Printer," this introductory edition printed the following table of contents at the top of the left-hand column:

OVERLAND MAIL

Important News from the United States
Oregon Question Settled---Defeat of
The Mexican Army---Official Report of
The movements of the American Army
At the Battle of the Rio Grande---
Santa Ana proclaimed President of
Mexcio!---Arrival of the" Fisguard, "
Capt. Dantze, from Puget Sound"[4]

Subsequently, Brannan published another extra edition On January 1, 1847. It primarily contained an open letter from Samuel Brannan to his fellow Saints in the United States and England and summarized the voyage on the *Brooklyn* and their experience since arriving at Yerba Buena and the establishment of the New Hope colony on the Stanislaus River. In the letter Brannan tells of anxiously awaiting the arrival of Saints coming by land, and urges: *"those wishing to emigrate to this Eldorado of the West"* to come by water in preference to land. Brannan also announced,

"We shall commence publishing a newspaper next week, which will be the government organ by sanction of Colonel Freemont [sic], who is now our Governor."[5]

The paper would not become a government organ, nor was Fremont the governor at the time. Brannan likely made those false claims to position a close, safe relationship with authorities and for his readers in the east and abroad.

The Acorn iron hand printing press, so-called because of its design, that Brannan had carefully shipped from New York, was commonly used by printers since the 1830s. It had been manufactured in the 1840s by Hoe & Co., of Boston, one of several manufacturers. A similar press from the Smith Company of New England had printed the original *Book of Mormon*.[6] The iron frame was an improvement over earlier wooden presses, adding strength and durability, but the printing process was essentially the same as innovated by Gutenberg in the 15th century. A compositor set lines of individual lead letters backwards, from right to left, in a wooden frame or galley. When the entire page was set in a form, the type was inked evenly by using leather balls. A sheet of paper was placed on a hinged frame, set on top of the inked type and slid under a platen. The pressman pulled a long "devil's tail" handle which turned a screw or lever and brought pressure on the paper, creating an inked image. The printed sheet was removed, and the process repeated. It was slow work; an experienced printer could print perhaps a hundred sheets an hour. Within a few years, steam would automate the process, greatly increasing the production. There were no illustrations in *The California Star.* Copper engravings required a different press and photo engraving was yet to be available.

The first weekly edition of San Francisco's first newspaper, *The California Star,* appeared on January 9, 1847, though it listed its location as Yerba Buena. The staff box at the top of column one read:

THE CALIFORNIA STAR
A WEEKLY JOURNAL
Devoted to the liberties and Interests of the

William Briggs

People of California
Published by Samuel Brannan
Edited by E.P. Jones
TERMS
Ivariably [sic] in advance

One copy per annum---Cash $6.00
Two copies "-------------------" 10.00
[Advertising rates followed]⁷

The entire front page was devoted to news from the war front. Sub-headlines included *"Matamoras Taken Without Opposition," "Treatment of American Prisoners by the Mexicns* [sic]," and *"Annexation."* Most of it was more than six months old, however this demonstrates the hunger of readers for war news. The Mexican War became the first war in history to be widely covered by journalists or correspondents, and which made use of the new telegraphic technology. However, in the 1840s, telegraph service had not extended across North America. News traveled to Yerba Buena as fast as riders on horseback could spur their mounts or settlers drive their wagons. More often communication travelled on arriving ships, taking several months from the east coast of America. Rather than sail around the Horn of South America as the *Brooklyn* had done, the distance and time could be shortened somewhat by crossing the Isthmus of Panama. But this travel incurred considerably more expense and still took many weeks. Nevertheless, the news-hungry readers of Yerba Buena eagerly consumed Brannan's first issue and promised success for the venture. Coincidentally, the last article on page four was a paragraph reprinted from the *Washington Union,* dated June

2nd, about the completion of a telegraph line between Washington and New York.

On the second page of edition no. 1, Elbert P. Jones introduced himself as the temporary editor of *The California Star* and promised to edit the paper solely in the interest of the public and without any *"private pique, personal feelings and jealousy."* He did not always live up to those goals. One reason Brannan tabbed Jones to edit the paper was his somewhat facility with the Spanish language. On the back page, printed in both English and Spanish was a proclamation from R.F. Stockton, Commander-in-Chief, and Governor of the Territory of California. In it, Stockton tells of U.S. defeat of Mexico at the Battle of La Mesa and the occupation of Los Angeles. He wrote:

> *"The flag of the United States is now flying from every commanding positions* [sic] *in the Territory, and California is entirely free from Mexican Dominion.*

> *"The Territory of California now belongs to the United States and will be governed as soon as circumstances may permit, by officers and laws similar to those by which the other Territories of the United States are regulated and protected.*

> *"But until the Governor, the Secretary and the Council are appointed, and the various civil departments of the Government are arranged, military laws will prevail, and the Commander-in-Chief will be the Governor and Protector of the Territory."*[8]

Thus, with publication in Brannan's *Star,* Governor Stockton's declaration of martial law placed California officially in the possession of the United States. The Treaty of Guadalupe Hidalgo, which followed the Mexican War, would be a formality. Brannan must have wondered at this point if Brigham Young would ever bring his followers to California and thus back into the United States.

The advent of the new newspaper in Yerba Buena did not go unnoticed by its Monterey counterpart. *The Californian* described it as a *"small but very neat sheet,"* and acknowledged Brannan's qualifications within his Mormon community. On the other hand, *Star* editor Jones forgot his pledge to keep his personal feelings out of his writing and called the Monterey paper a *"dim, dirty little rag"* and its editors *"a lying sycophant and the other an overgrown lickspittle."*[9] From the onset, these editors instituted the climate of petty jealousies and sniping between rival publications that became a hallmark of the newspaper industry.

By the second edition on January 16th, the *Star* had found its footing. It published a strongly worded editorial, written by Jones but no doubt echoing publisher Brannan, on the subject of press freedom. Referencing and repeating the First Amendment of the U.S. Constitution, it directly challenged what was seen as governmental abridgement of that freedom:

> *"It is with deepest sorrow and regret that we have witnessed what we believed to be an attempt to interfere with it* [press freedom] *here...Military laws cannot affect the press or anyone concerned in carrying it on; because all the military laws are made by Congress, and by the Constitution,*

Congress is prohibited from making any law abridging the freedom of the press. "[10]

This tension between guaranteed personal freedoms of speech and religion and actual practice had underscored the entire Latter-Day Saint experience, of which press freedom would be but a small example. If the Mormons were to settle in an American California, Brannan would use the power of the press to preclude what he saw as the same governmental overreach that had driven his people from the United States already.

On that same page of the second edition, the *Star* reported the following story under the headline *Emigrants in the Mountains:*

> *"It is probably not generally known to people, that there is mow in the California Mountains in a most distressing situation, a party of emigrants from the United States, who were prevented from crossing the mountains by an early heavy fall of snow. The party consists of about sixty persons, men, women and children. They were almost entirely out of provisions, when they reached the foot of the mountain, but for the timely succor afforded them by Capt. J.A. Sutter, one of the most humane and liberal men in California, they must have all perished in a few days. Captain Sutter as soon as he ascertained their situation, sent five mules loaded with provisions to them. A second party was dispatched with provisions for them, but they found the mountain impassable, in consequence of the*

*snow. We hope that our citizens will do something
for the relief of these unfortunate people."*[11]

This, of course, was the breaking news of the tragedy
endured by the Donner Party. In subsequent issues, *The Star*
would follow the story and provide readers – and the nation –
with details of the horrors faced by those emigrants in the
Sierra winter, including graphic descriptions of cannibalism.
Mormon men joined the efforts to rescue the stranded
emigrants still alive during February and March 1847. Sam
Brannan spearheaded a fundraising drive among his
community for relief of the surviving Donners.

On the back page of that same edition, publisher Brannan
told his readers:

*"Being anxious to secure to himself and the
citizens of his adopted country* [California]*, the
benefits of a free, fearless and untrammalled* [sic]
*Newspaper – Purchased and brought with him to
California a press and all the materials necessary
to effect that desirable object. Contrary to our
original intention* [an internal Mormon publication]
*but being fully convinced the present crisis in the
affairs of the country demands it, we have resolved
to commence at ONCE the publication of a paper
to be styled THE CALIFORNIA STAR."*[12]

With publication of the third edition, *The California Star*
was engaging in a dialogue with readers submitting letters to
the editor. Many of these were signed with pseudonyms, a long
newspapering tradition. In addition to reprinting a few articles
from earlier editions and some articles written in Spanish, *The*

Star published a small notice submitted by *Alcalde* Washington Bartlett that would prove of dramatic, lasting importance:

AN ORDINANCE

Whereas the local name of Yerba Buena as applied to the settlement of San Francisco – is unknown beyond the immediate district; and has been applied from the local name of the Cove on which the town is built – Therefore to prevent confusion and mistakes in public documents, and that the town may have the advantage of the name given on the published maps.

It is hereby ordered that the name of San Francisco shall hereafter be used in all official communications and public documents, or records appertaining to this town.

Wash'n A. Bartlett
Chief Magistrate[13]

In a single, unilateral decision, Mayor Bartlett had officially baptized the town San Francisco forever, relegating the name Yerba Buena to the margins and to history. The actual reason behind this abrupt decision had less to do with public documents and maps and more to do with competition with another emerging township on San Francisco Bay and the ambition of a trio of municipal rivals.

Following his arrest during the Bear Flag Revolt, *Alta* California *Comandante General* Mariano Guadalupe Vallejo spent time as a prisoner of John C. Fremont in Sutter's Fort. During his incarceration he suffered from a bout of malaria and agreed to remain neutral in the conflict between Mexico and the United States. A well-educated Mexican *don* fluent in

English, Vallejo had amassed enormous land holdings through Mexican land grants following secularization of mission lands in the 1830s. In addition to his 44,000-acre Rancho Petaluma, he had laid out the town of Sonoma. However, having received land in lieu of money for his services from the Mexican government, Vallejo needed income. Reading the prevailing political winds, in a jailhouse conversion, Vallejo came to believe the best interests of California rested with the United States, not Mexico.

Having received more than 125,000 square miles of land from the Mexican government, Vallejo sought to develop land to create income. In 1846, Vallejo approached U.S. Consul Thomas O. Larkin and Robert Semple, the Monterey business entrepreneur (and newspaper editor) with his plan to develop a new township on the north bank of the Carquinez Straits in San Francisco Bay. Semple had been instrumental in the Bear Flag Revolt and had been responsible for transporting Vallejo to Sutter's Fort where the two became friends. Semple and Larkin were impressed with Vallejo's vision and the site's potential. Robert Semple began to promote the concept of the new city in his Monterey newspaper, hoping to attract investors. Vallejo would provide the land with the stipulation that the new town be named after his wife, Francisca Benicia Carillo de Vallejo. It was to be called Francisca.[14.] On January 19, 1847, Vallejo *et. al.* filed paperwork for the new town with Alcalde Bartlett.

In Yerba Buena, *Alcalde* Bartlett and Samuel Brannan both sensed the threat such a development posed to their young community. Although The village of Yerba Buena was not known as San Francisco, the great bay had long been designated San Francisco Bay on maps and in popular usage.

Naming this proposed new town *"Francisca"* was not only confusingly too similar, but also would divert future shipping and commerce away from Yerba Buena, which would then remain nothing more than a sleepy back-water with limited growth potential. On the other hand, if Yerba Buena was officially linked to San Francisco, the business would flow their way. Bartlett moved quickly to steal Vallejo's thunder, monopolizing the name in a deft move of semantic tyranny. It proved prophetic. While San Francisco would evolve into a major city and world-class port, the other town, ultimately to be called Benicia, Vallejo's second choice after his wife's middle name, while a bustling port of its own for river and bay shipping, and even state capital for a year in the 1850s, never emerged from the shadow of San Francisco.

Not everyone applauded the choice to focus on San Francisco. William Tecumseh Sherman, the young Army officer stationed in California during the Mexican War and later noted Civil War general, groused:

> *"That Benicia was the best natural site for a commercial city I am satisfied and had half the money and half the labor been bestowed on it that had been spent on San Francisco, we should this day have a city of palaces on the Carquinez Straits."*[15]

Although a party to the christening of their town from the beginning, Sam Brannan did not change the masthead of *The California Star* from Yerba Buena to San Francisco until the edition of March 20th when he wrote:

"Our readers will perceive that in our present number we have conformed to the change recently made in the name of our town, by placing at the head of our paper SAN FRANCISCO instead of YERBA BUENA. The change has now been made legally and we aquiese [sic] in it, though we prefer the old name – the one by which the place has always been known in this country."[16]

Brannan went on to regularly impugn the integrity and honor of William Bartlett. Nevertheless, Samuel Brannan will forever share the honor, responsibility or blame for naming The City San Francisco.

The California Star maintained its weekly publication schedule without interruption for the rest of 1847 with little modification to layout or content. Edition 51 would be published on Christmas Day, 1847. The volume of advertising slowly increased as the business community evolved. By summer, Brannan had moved business card display ads to the front page. In April, Jones's name had been removed from the staff box and the cantankerous editor had been unceremoniously removed from the newspaper office. He would immediately be replaced by Edward C. Kemble, though the announcement was withheld until fall after Brannan's journey to meet with Brigham Young. Despite his absence, the editorial transition went smoothly, and the paper would not miss a deadline. San Francisco was a newspaper town.

Notes

1. Edward Kemble , *Sacramento Daily Union,* Sept. 16, 1871.

2. _____, "Twenty Years Ago, *"Sacramento Daily Union,* September 11, 1866.

3. G.S. Breschini, "The First Newspaper in California," Monterey County Historical Society, 2000, http://mchmuseum.com>firstpaper, retrieved Dec. 29, 2022.

4. *An EXTRA IN ADVANCE OF THE CALIFORNIA STAR,* Oct. 21, 1846.

5. S. Brannan, "TO THE SAINTS IN ENGLAND AND AMERICA,' *the California Star Extra,* Jan. 1, 1847.

6. Floyd D.P. Oydegaard, "The Acorn Press. Where is it Today?," *Columbia Gazette,* Columbia State Historic Park, http://www.columbiagazette.com>acorn, retrieved Feb. 20, 2023. Following the Gold Rush, A press long-thought to be Brannan's made its way through the foothills of the Sierra to Marysville, Auburn and Columbia. It eventually ended in care of the National Park Service, loaned to Sutter's Fort, the Oakland Museum and widely displayed throughout Northern California, including the courthouse in Auburn as late as 2006. However, the original Brannan press likely was destroyed in an 1851 Sacramento fire.

7. *The California Star,* January 9, 1847.

8. Ibid.

9. Fred Blackburn Rogers, <u>The California Star</u>, Berkeley, CA: Howell-North Books, 1965, p. vii.

10. The California Star, January 16, 1847.

11. Ibid.

12. Ibid.

13. Ibid.

14. "Founders of Benicia 1847," History Makers Database, https://www.hmdb.org, retrieved Feb. 11, 2023.

15. Ibid.

16. *The California Star,* op. cit., March 20, 1847.

Illustrations

William Briggs

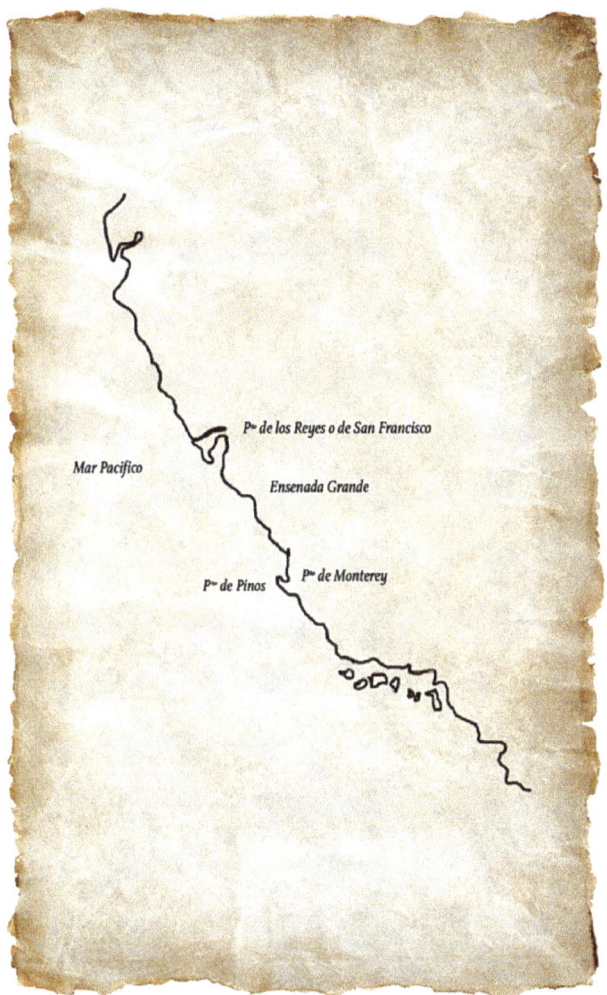

Vizcaino Map, 1602.

Detail from Sebastian Vizcaino's map of the California coastline from Monterey to Point Reyes, 1602. The small indentation of *Ensenada Grande* was one of the earliest depictions of yet-undiscovered San Francisco Bay.

Illustration by Briana Monaco

The Portola Expedition Views San Francisco Bay, Nov. 4, 1769.

Painting by Mort Kunstler (1969).

Copyright © San Mateo County Historical Association (1976.264).

Count Nicolai Rezanov

The Russian diplomat was one of the first foreign visitors to San Francisco Bay, in 1806.

Wikipedia – Public Domain.

Presidio of San Francisco, c. 1850.

Etching by unknown artist, National Archives and Records Administration.

National Park Service – Public Domain.

Mission of Los Dolores, c. 1850-1854.

By G.R. Fardon. Some passengers from the *Brooklyn* found shelter at the old Franciscan mission.

SMU Central Libraries, Flickr's Commons – Public Domain.

View of San Francisco, formerly Yerba Buena, 1846-7.

Yerba Buena Cove as it would have appeared to the arriving passengers on the *Brooklyn*. *USS Portsmouth* is anchored in foreground.

Wikimedia Commons – Public Domain.

Ship *Brooklyn* off Skerries Rock.

Painting by Duncan McFarlane (1834-1871).

Wikipedia – Public Domain.

Map of the Voyage of the *Brooklyn*, 1846.

Illustration by Briana Monaco.

Portrait of Samuel Brannan.
Wikimedia Commons – Public Domain.

Portrait of Edward Kemble.

Boy editor of *The California Star*. Kemble became the Father of California Journalism.

Courtesty of California Press Foundation. Original Source unknown.

Original Office Site of *The California Star*.

Located just off the old Yerba Buena Plaza in today's Chinatown, Sam Brannan's house also served as the site of San Francisco's first newspaper.

Author's photograph.

Acorn Printing Press.

Stereoscope of Gold-Rush-era Acorn Printing press. The original Sam Brannan press was likely destroyed in an 1851 Sacramento fire.

Keystone View Co. photography, 1925.

U.C. Riverside ARTS, California Museum of Photography.

An Early Newspaper Office.

By Anton Refregier (between 1946-48)
Original at Rincon Center, San Francisco.

Part of a series of WPA-sponsored public art depicting
San Francisco history. The figure is assumed to be
Samuel Brannan.

U.S. Library of Congress, Prints and Photographs Division
– Public Domain

Portrait of Brigham Young, c. 1853.

Daguerreotype of Mormon leader who rejected Brannan's urging to colonize California with the Latter-Day Saints.

Wikimedia Commons – Public Domain.

Sutter's Fort (Reconstruction).

Sutter's Fort State Historic Park, Sacramento, CA.

Author's photograph.

Sutter's Mill (Reconstruction).

James Marshall Discovery Site, Coloma, CA.

Photograph courtesy Brian Ugie.

San Francisco, 1849.

Engraving – artist unknown.

U.S. Library of Congress – Public Domain.

Yerba Buena Harbor, 1850 or 1851.

Daguerreotype – photographer unknown.

Yerba Buena (Goat) Island in background

U.S. Library of Congress – Public Domain.

Portsmouth Square During Gold Rush, 1851.

Note *Alta California* office over print shop. Original site of *The Californian* newspaper on hilltop, right, with windmill.

U.S. Library of Congress – Public Domain.

Panorama of San Francisco Today.

From Coit Tower on Telegraph Hill (left) to the Transamerica Pyramid (right), as seen from Ina Coolbrith Park, Taylor and Vallejo Streets. The lower profile area with some red brick buildings just before the bay in the middle distance was once Yerba Buena.

Author's photograph.

Chapter 7
Bay or Lake?

"Within a few years the wealth and influence of this place could be entirely received to our interest."

– Samuel Brannan, December 5, 1847

"We have no business in San Francisco."

– Brigham Young, 1847

Establishing *The Star* was by no means Brannan's only priority in those first months in California. As shepherd of his flock of Latter-Day Saints, he busied himself officiating at weekly religious services, held in the Customs House. He delivered the first English language sermon and performed the first non-Catholic marriage in California. As he had done on the *Brooklyn,* he again exercised his religious authority by excommunicating a score of men who had wandered away from the faith, for which he was later unsuccessfully sued. Legal troubles had entangled Brannan since their arrival, when a military court investigated the motives and loyalties of the new arrivals. That fall, Brannan was also sued over the legality of his contract of "limited communism," the pooling of the group's resources under Brannan's management. Through a career of defending himself in courts, ecclesiastical, civil and military, Sam Brannan avoided convictions by what we today call "Teflon coating," though his lifelong affairs in business, the Church and his personal relationships with women or the bottle certainly tainted his reputation along the way.

One motive for the frenzy of activity during the first months at Yerba Buena was the anticipation of large numbers of their brothers and sisters soon joining them on the Pacific coast. Brannan had been told a second ship of Saints would follow *The Brooklyn*. At the same time, thousands of Saints were following Brigham Young across the Great Plains, and the bounty and climate of California made it the logical destination to establish their New Zion. To that end, it fell to Brannan to ensure Yerba Buena would be prepared to welcome these legions of pilgrims. Although food was plentiful for his own small company – beef from the *ranchos* and game from the surrounding woods were abundant – but it would take a miracle to provide enough loaves and fishes to feed the expected multitudes.

To meet the anticipated food requirements, Brannan dispatched a dozen colonists inland to establish a farming station. In an open converted whaleboat called *Comet*, the party sailed up the San Joaquín River just beyond its confluence with the Stanislaus River, and in the delta laid out a new settlement called New Hope, some seventy miles from Yerba Buena. They carried with them some rudimentary farm implements and seed for planting wheat and potatoes. A team of oxen would be driven to the site by land. The group constructed log cabins and planted some eighty acres of wheat and vegetables. The entire venture would be owned by S. Brannan & Co., further exacerbating the discontent over Brannan's dictatorial control and seeming conflicts of interest with his role as church leader. Brannan's enterprise also bought city lots and constructed buildings on speculation. Many of the colonists resented working to put money in Brannan's hands, and several drifted away from the settlement. The San Joaquín delta was prone to annual flooding and the marshy land was prime breeding ground for mosquitoes and their curse, malaria. Winter floods washed away much of the planted seed and the first harvest was dismal. Despite best intentions and best efforts, the New Hope Colony ended in failure and would be disbanded in a year's time.

In February 1847, Sam Brannan wrote a letter of encouragement to the dozen or so colonists still at New Hope, while clearly thinking about next steps in case of failure:

> *"I hope you will not get discouraged, but press onward and trust in God, and that the strong will not be overcome by the faint-hearted...if God wants to destroy our crop of wheat up their [sic] let his will be done not ours – he knows what is best, better than we – and he has the helm – and will do just what is right. Have your horses ready and we will go to the mountains and see the Indians without fail."*[1]

Meanwhile, Brannan became increasingly anxious about being reinforced by the large party of Latter-Day Saints. He had received no communication from Brigham Young since leaving New York and had no idea how far the land party had progressed across the continent. After several months in California, Brannan was even more convinced it should become the Saints' new home. But the thought that Brigham Young may think otherwise nagged at him and he needed to be sure. He decided to personally intercept Young enroute, wherever he would find him, convince the Church president California was the promised land prophesized by Joseph Smith, and lead them back over the Sierra to Yerba Buena. With New Hope at least initially established, he turned to his newspaper and handed the editorial reins to his protégé, Edward Kemble, all before leaving for his Stanley-meets-Livingston quest to locate Brigham Young somewhere in North America.

Not even his wife, who steadfastly denied the realities of living in California, held greater insight into the thoughts and deeds of Sam Brannan than Edward C. Kemble. He was, variously, Brannan's assistant, sounding board, confidant and mouthpiece through *The Star,* though he professed never having been of the Mormon faith. Kemble was born in 1828 into a family that mixed politics and journalism. His father had been a New York state senator and newspaper editor. His maternal great grandfather had signed the Declaration of Independence. Young Kemble had apprenticed to Brannan at the *New York Messenger* and had been intrigued enough or sufficiently adventurous to make the long voyage with his boss.

Shortly after arrival of the *Brooklyn,* Colonel John C. Fremont rode into Yerba Buena recruiting soldiers for his mounted California Battalion. Several Mormons were eager to enlist until the presence of many Missourians in the battalion caused the Mormons to turn away, refusing to serve with men from the state where their faith had been persecuted and expelled. Edward Kemble was not dissuaded, however, and signed on with K Company. In November, Kemble was involved in the Battle of Natividad in the Salinas Valley, a skirmish that allowed Fremont to continue his march into southern California. Kemble remained with Fremont's forces as they next occupied Santa Barbara without resistance. By the following January, the combined naval and army forces under Commodore Robert F. Stockton and Brigadier Stephen W. Kearny had defeated the army of Mexicans and *Californios* at San Gabriel River and La Mesa before entering Los Angeles and ending fighting in Alta California. On January 13, 1847, Fremont brokered the Treaty of Cahuenga with Andres Pico, without official approval of either government – that was Fremont's style – but the fighting in California was nevertheless over. By September, U.S. forces had occupied Mexico City, Mexican President Santa Ana had resigned, and the war ended. In February 1848, the Treaty of Guadalupe-Hidalgo formally ceded Alta California to the United States. Young Kemble, still shy of his 20th birthday, had meanwhile been discharged with rank of sergeant, returned to Yerba Buena and become "boy editor" of *The California Star.*

Brannan quietly slipped out of town in spring 1847. He stopped to visit the members hanging on at New Hope before arriving at Sutter's Fort to supply himself for the journey east to find Young. In what would be his final communique with original editor E. P. Jones before Jones was replaced by Kemble, Brannan sent a report from Sutter's Fort, outlining his views on some matters of veterans' pay and some issues of Indian affairs. Jones would not be around to publish Brannan's report. Circumspect, almost clandestine, Brannan had added a postscript:

> *"P.S. I shall start the last of this week across the mountains – give my respects to all enquiring friends – Kimbell* [Kemble] *can read my writing*

but it may want some corrections, yours respectfully,

"S. Brannan"[2]

Brannan, fearful that Jones would take advantage of his absence and write irresponsible editorials, had prearranged with Kemble to remove the feisty Tennessee lawyer if need be. After Kemble threw him out, Jones abandoned newspaper work and became highly successful in real estate development before leaving California by 1850. Kemble and another printer off the *Brooklyn* named John Eager (son of the excommunicated Lucy Eager) would operate *The Star* until Brannan's return from Salt Lake, at which time Kemble was officially elevated to editor.

Brannan, accompanied by three other men and saddle and pack horses, left Sutter's Fort on April 26th and headed into the Sierra, still blanketed with winter snow. Ascending the west side of the mountains, they passed through the abandoned camp of the Donners, still littered with human remains, evidence of their desperate acts of survival. Months later, at Fort Hall (in modern Idaho) he wrote an abbreviated summary of his journey to an associate in New York, G.T. Newell, who published it in the *Millennial Star*:

> *"We crossed the Snowy Mountains of California, a distance of forty miles, with eleven head of horse and mules, in one day and two hours, a thing that had never been done before in less than three days....During our journey, we have endured many hardships and fatigues in swimming rivers, and climbing mountains, not being able to travel the regular route owing to the high waters. Had I time*

and paper I might give you quite an interesting account of the country and our travels throughout."[3]

Once through the pass in the High Sierra, Brannan's party followed the evolving emigrant trail northeast across the Great Basin to the Green River, west of South Pass in today's Wyoming, where he encountered the advance party of overland Saints on June 30th.

Earlier that month, Brigham Young had written a letter to Sam Brannan updating the California Mormons on the progress of the main party crossing the plains and inquiring about affairs in California. The letter was never sent for lack of means of communication but was saved for posterity. He described his advance party as being comprised of some 200 men, while he expected that some 4,000 Saints had by then left Winter Quarters on the Missouri River and were enroute to join the vanguard. Young passed along greetings and news from several mutual acquaintances and observed,

> *"The papers report your safe arrival* [at Yerba Buena] *and that you have the only Printing Office in Upper California, but we do not know the name of your paper but hope to see* [it] *at the first opportunity, though I don't expect to see this scribble in type, it is only for your eye, and blunders are always excusable among old friends."*[4]

Interestingly, Young told Brannan, *"The camp will not go to the West Coast or to your place at present, they do not have the means."*[5.] The Saints were certainly cash poor as well as exhausted by their trek. However, this excuse may have masked an earlier decision Young had made about California.

The meeting between Samuel Brannan and Brigham Young was civil, cordial at best rather than warm. For several days Brannan extolled the benefits of California, painting this *El Dorado* as the ideal location for their Tribe of Israel to settle. Brannan was an eloquent speaker and a capable advocate for his cause. Brigham Young listened with patience. After a few days, Brannan was sent on a scouting errand to meet some returning veterans from the Mormon Battalion, while Young pushed into the Valley of the Great Salt Lake. Days later, Brannan returned and accompanied Young and other church leaders on a reconnaissance of the area.

On July 28, many of the pioneers gathered around Brigham Young, who had already determined that location to be the site of their new Jerusalem. In a gesture that would become almost mythologized within Church history, Young struck the ground with his cane and publicly declared it the site for their new temple, as affirmed, he emphasized, in a vision. There was no dissent. Among the gathered, Brannan, for once, stood speechless. His arguments had proved futile, his dreams for California dashed, his journey for naught. Brannan thought Brigham Young daft for opting to settle in an arid desert adjoining a saline lake even birds avoided, instead of fertile, welcoming California. But he recognized Young was stubbornly determined and there would be no change of mind. Brigham Young is reported to have told him the place for the Saints was together in the Utah desert, not among the gentiles who would increasingly be drawn to the richness of California. If they went to California, Young remarked, they would stay five years; if they built at Salt Lake they would stay forever. Brannan believed the venture at Salt Lake would fail. A week later, Samuel Brannan began his return trip to California, discouraged and disillusioned. Before departing, Brannan also denounced the practice of polygamy to Young, who met the rebuke with stony silence. Brigham Young's decision would alter the character and destiny of San Francisco, and events of the following year would transform The City forever.

Samuel Brannan returned to San Francisco a changed man. While his faith had not wavered, his zeal had been blunted. He brought with him a pair of letters from Brigham Young. The first, an open letter to the Saints in California, reaffirmed Brannan's role as president of the Church in California, but the tepid endorsement damned Brannan with faint praise and obliquely alluded to complaints he had heard about Brannan's leadership:

> *"Bretheren and sisters, we feel to say to you, that we are satisfied with your mission which you have taken to California, & that so far as we have been informed, we are satisfied with the proceedings of Elder Brannan. We believe that he is a good man & that it is his design to do right. No doubt he has been placed in very trying circumstances in connection & common with you, since your journey to California was first contemplated; & if he or you have erred in anything, in the midst of your trials & troubles it is nothing more than others have done before you, & nothing more than is expected of man while he is so imperfect as he now."*[6]

After a lengthy summary of the overland trek, Young described the settlement planned for the Salt Lake Basin, making it clear that it, not California, was to be their home:

William Briggs

*"To all the Saints in California, you are in a
goodly land; & if you choose to tarry where you
are, you are at liberty to so to do; & if you choose
to come to this place* [Salt Lake], *you are at liberty
to come, & we shall be happy to receive you, &
give you an inheritance in our midst; And if any
emigrants should arrive upon the Western Shores,
let no one discourage them from coming to this
place, if they wish to do so; not that we wish to
depopulate California of all the Saints, but that we
wish to make this a Stronghold, a rallying point, a
more immediate gathering place than any other; &
from hence let the work go out, and in* [the] *process
of time the Shores of the Pacific may be overlooked
from the Temple of the Lord* [i.e. from Salt Lake
City]. "*[7]*

Brigham Young further undermined Latter-Day Saint
concentration in California by discouraging their public
displays of religious practice, ostensibly to avoid confusion,
but more likely to make California less religiously attractive to
his highly spiritual followers. He also instructed his followers
not to publicize the virtues of Salt Lake to those outside the
faith.

During this brief sojourn to the Utah desert to meet
Brigham Young, San Francisco had changed as well. Though
Brannan would report he found things upon return better than
"his sanguine expectations," in fact some things had
deteriorated. By that September the farm community at New
Hope had failed. Although President Young had tacitly
endorsed the temporary non-Mormon practice of communal

economics as a means justifying a desired end, mounting dissatisfaction with Brannan's management brought about the dissolution of S. Brannan & Co., by the end of that month, though Brannan retained the venture's assets, including the land. The summons by Brigham Young and the knowledge that the main party of Saints would not be coming to California motivated several of the *Brooklyn* company to pack up and head to Salt Lake, eager to rejoin their friends, relatives and the rest of the host there. Dissension was further heightened by the arrival of several members of the Mormon Battalion, having been discharged that summer in southern California at the end of their enlistment, following conclusion of hostilities with Mexico. These veterans, equally disciplined by the Church and the Army, rejected allegiance to the local Mormon leader.

On the other hand, San Francisco's population had grown to nearly 500 inhabitants. *The California Star* was thriving, serving the community's hunger for news and its yearlong campaign for a schoolhouse bore fruit with the town's first school on Clay Street in December 1847:

> *"The new School House is at length completed and at the disposal of the authorities of San Francisco…It is unnecessary to remind our authorities that a competent English teacher is yet to be secured. School Commissioners should be appointed, and the necessary arrangements made for the organization of a school forthwith."*[8]

Several new buildings had been constructed and the town had prospered by selling numerous plots of land at a substantial profit, including the curious "water lots," property normally submerged in the tidal basin, except at lowest tides.

Originally, the beach front was considered public land, until Governor Kearny authorized municipal leaders to claim it and use as a revenue source. Some 444 50-*vara* lots were auctioned off. Speculators, such as Brannan, bought these water lots and moved closest to the anchoring ships, building wharves and warehouses on piers out into the bay. In time, this area (including modern Green, Front, Fremont, and Folsom streets) would be filled in, creating some of San Francisco's most desirable real estate (and most susceptible to liquification during an earthquake).

Brannan remained active in his role as Church leader, committed to the idea that Mormons would prosper in California. But increasingly, he found himself dealing with the growing gentile population, entering business deals and partnerships and plunging deeper into civic affairs. He became open to a more secular, less disciplined lifestyle. As his attention was drawn away from the *Brooklyn* Saints more and more, their criticism grew in proportion. His vision for California was changing to a broader future, played out on a larger scale. Soon, the temptations of that wider world and his associations in it would prove irresistible, and the tsunami building toward California would soon figuratively inundate San Francisco.

Notes

1. Samuel Brannan, letter to E.P. Jones, April 18, 1847, Elbert P. Jones Papers, Bancroft Library.

2. Samuel Brannan, letter to G.T. Newell, June 18, 1847, published in *Latter-Day Saints Millennial Star,* Oct. 15, 1847.

3. Brigham Young, unsent letter to Samuel Brannan, June 6, 1847.

4. Ibid.

5. Brigham Young, letter To the Saints in California, Aug. 7, 1847, Special Collections, BYU Library.

6. Ibid.

7. Samuel Brannan, letter to the Brethren at New Hope, Feb. 13, 1847, LDS Archives.

8. *The California Star,* Dec. 4, 1847.

William Briggs

Chapter 8
Sutter's Secret

"Such was life in the Golden Gate:
Gold dusted all we drank and ate."

– Robert Frost,
West-Running Brook, 1928

A s Sam Brannan and his traveling companions had returned from their encounter with Brigham Young at the Great Salt Lake, they had encountered several groups of recently discharged Mormon Battalion veterans heading east along the California Trail over Donner Pass in the Sierra. Some of these men had been among the first to find the grizzly remains of the Donner Party victims, and the veterans had provided a solemn burial party for the dead. With each group they met, Brannan expressed his disappointment that Young had decided against bringing the Saints to California. Traveling with Brannan, Captain James Brown carried a missive from the Mormon leader to the returning veterans. Young would gladly welcome them back into the bosom of the Saints and share their happiness at reuniting with their families, but at the same time, fearing for food shortage in the Salt Lake Valley, he encouraged those without means to remain in California through the winter. While about half of the veterans still pushed on, the rest turned around and headed back into the Sacramento Valley and many of them made for Sutter's Fort.

During the Mexican War, the Mormon Battalion had endured one of the longest military marches in history. They had marched from Fort Leavenworth on the Missouri River to Santa Fe before covering another thousand miles across inhospitable terrain and burning desert from New Mexico to California, under the command of Brevet Lt. Colonel Philip St. George Cooke, a veteran of the Black Hawk War. On the long march, the battalion had encountered no enemy troops, although a skirmish at Tucson had been narrowly avoided by the Mexicans retreating. By the time of their arrival in California, the fighting there was over. The Mormon Battalion arrived footsore and malnourished at San Diego and welcomed the sight of the Pacific Ocean. As occupation troops for duration of their enlistment, the battalion was assigned light duty completing public works and constructing forts at Los Angeles and the Tejon Pass.

Upon discharge on their enlistment anniversary date of July 16, 1847, some 80 veterans opted to reenlist. A small detachment accompanied John Fremont to Washington to stand his court martial for his insubordination with General Kearny over Fremont's claim to the governorship, despite Kearny's superior rank. The remainder of the battalion began to make their way north through the San Joaquín Valley, planning to eventually reunite with the Saints gathering at Salt Lake. A smaller number under Captain Jefferson Hunt journeyed north along the old *El Camino Real* coastal mission trail to Monterey and San Francisco, or on to Sutter's Fort in the Sacramento

Valley, to obtain the supplies needed for the journey across the Sierra to Utah.

In May 1847, Jefferson Hunt had written to Brigham Young, asking the leader for direction:

> *"In two months, we look for a discharge and know not whether to stick our course. We have a very good offer to purchase a large valley sufficient to support 50,000 families, connected with other excellent country which might be obtained...We may have the land and stock, consisting of eight thousand head of cattle."*[1]

Clearly, Captain Hunt was enchanted by the possibilities of remaining in California, but Brigham Young had already made his decision. By summer, these Mormon Battalion veterans would learn of Young's arrival at Salt Lake and his announcement that would be the place to build their Zion. Regrouping at Sutter's Fort, the "battalion boys" had their own decision to make: either obtain sufficient supplies to continue on to Salt Lake immediately before winter; heed Young's admonition to seek temporary employment in California before returning the following spring; or remain in California and buildi a new life there.

As many as 60 veterans opted to remain in California over-winter and approached Captain John Sutter about employment. With the American annexation of California, Sutter faced prospects of the collapse of his agricultural empire. As a hedge against calamity, Sutter busily diversified his enterprises, planning to construct a gristmill not far from the fort and a sawmill some 40 miles upstream on the south fork of the American River at a place the Native Americans called Coloma. Sutter enthusiastically grabbed the opportunity to employ so many skilled and semi-skilled workers, including blacksmiths, carpenters and disciplined, strong, common laborers. And best, the Mormon Battalion veterans were already organized and willing to work for either cash or supplies and mounts for their proposed trip across the Sierra, payment of which could be deferred until spring.

Captain Sutter was not the only one diversifying his affairs. In San Francisco, Sam Brannan's problems with the Church continued. He sought to deflect criticism by lecturing his congregation on the disaffection running rife within their community. He challenged his detractors to come forward with their charges against him. Having liquidated the communal S. Brannan & Co., despite Brigham Young's counsel to the contrary, Sam Brannan wrote to Brigham Young, asking for *"confidence, faith and prayers"* in the discharge of his duties, and offered *"to render an account* of [his] *stewardship."*[2.] Next, Brannan moved to reorganize the San Francisco Branch of the Church, shifting its presidency to Addison Pratt, who then refused to act as Brannan's surrogate. By devoting less time to Church business, Brannan was able to pursue his own business interests.

Brannan was drawn into the orbit of John Sutter and the two men developed a close relationship, each believing in the potential of the Sacramento Valley. Sutter encouraged Brannan to establish a mercantile operation in the developing community around his fort. With his contacts in San Francisco, Brannan could control the entire supply chain from bay ports to a general merchandise store at the fort and monopolize sales to local merchants and the growing number of immigrants. Sutter, himself, would be Brannan's biggest customer and offered to provide space for the enterprise. Brannan quickly sought out a wealthy trader named Charles C. Smith, and together they opened a business in a building previously used as a hospital in the shadow of Sutter's walls. He acquired a large inventory of military surplus equipment at deeply discounted cost. Providing clothing, hardware and supplies for those packing across the Sierra, the business flourished from the start. Sam Brannan was building his first fortune and incrementally declaring his independence from the influence – if not yet the beliefs – of the Church of Jesus Christ of Latter-Day Saints.

For John Sutter, the battalion veterans seemed to answer his financial prayers. He claimed they were the best workers he'd ever employed. By their efforts he reasoned the gristmill would soon be completed and turn a profit, allowing him to pay down his substantial debt to the Russians for the purchase of their Fort Ross holdings. He wrote to both Mariano Vallejo in Sonoma and Thomas Larkin in Monterey, boasting how his Mormon workers at his new tannery were turning out large numbers of hides, and even producing quality-made shoes. New Helvetia was showing a good return. Given the strong demand for lumber in San Francisco and the Sacramento Valley, the soon-to-be completed sawmill on the American River would push the profits even higher. But John Sutter's world would flip upside down with events at the sawmill's construction site in January 1848.

Sutter's search for the perfect location for his sawmill had been interrupted by the events of the Mexican War, but as northern California settled down, Sutter moved aggressively to complete the project. He selected the Coloma site because it provided countless stands of tall, straight Ponderosa pine for lumber and sufficient water to power the mill, all within reasonable distance and access from his fort. He was approached by an unemployed failed farmer from New Jersey named James W. Marshall, who offered his millwright and carpentry skills to Sutter in return for a partnership in the proposed mill. Sutter agreed to supply the work crew and necessary building materials for Marshall to oversee the construction and operation of the mill. Together they would share the future profits. It was a risky speculative venture. Both men were hugely in debt. The work crew consisted of several Mormon Battalion veterans willing to defer their wages until the mill was operational, as well as several local Nisenan Native Americans, hired to do the heavy lifting. If the venture failed, all concerned would suffer.

Work progressed through the fall of 1847 and the sawmill was completed just after the turn of the new year. In a trial run, the diverted river easily turned the giant wheel, but the downstream millrace was too shallow to carry off the volume of water and the race backed up to the mill. James Marshall decided to use the flow of water to further erode and deepen the ditch. After letting the river run all night, Marshall closed the flood gates in the morning and examined the scoured ditch. The rushing water had carved out a channel and deposited a large measure of gravel and sand at the far end of the ditch. In the puddle, Marshall spotted some bright yellow flakes reflecting the early morning light. Years later, Marshall wrote his own account of his discovery:

"One morning in January – it was a clear, cold morning; I shall never forget that morning, – as I was taking my usual walk along the race after shutting off the water, my eye was caught with the glimpse of something shining in the bottom of the ditch. There was about a foot of water running then. I reached my hand down and picked it up; it made my heart thump, for I was certain it was gold. The piece was about half the size and the shape of a pea. Then I saw another piece in the water. After taking it out I sat down and began to think right hard. I thought it was gold...Suddenly the idea flashed across my mind that it might be iron pyrites [fool's gold]. *I trembled to think of it! This question could soon be determined. Putting one of the pieces on a hard river stone, I took another and commenced hammering it. It was soft, and didn't break; it therefore must be gold, but largely mixed with some other metal, very likely silver; for pure gold, I thought, would certainly have a brighter color."*[3]

Marshall was still troubled by doubt as he showed the nuggets to his workmen, who were similarly puzzled. They subjected the sample to extreme heat, and it did not melt. Legend has it that Elizabeth "Jennie" Wimmer (or Weimer, the camp laundress and cook and wife of a non-Mormon supervising the Nisenan Indians named Peter Wimmer), put the nuggets in a vat of lye she was using to make soap. When retrieved, the nuggets had not changed. The camp excitedly believed Marshall had indeed found gold, though they believed it to be just a few flecks rather than a major strike. Nevertheless, Marshall swore the group to secrecy and turned his attention back to opening the sawmill. When not occupied in the operation of the mill, the workers scouted the nearby trace for more signs of gold. Soon each man had found a small amount. A week later, Marshall collected all the samples of gold and made the trip to Sutter's Fort.

In the privacy of Sutter's office, Marshall showed his partner his discovery. Sutter consulted his reference library and then subjected the samples to crude chemical analysis and measured its specific gravity. All tests yielded the same results: gold. According to Marshall, *"This fact being ascertained. We thought it our best policy to keep it as quiet as possible till we should have finished our mill."*[4]

Marshall returned to Coloma immediately, greeting his comrades with *"O boys, it is the pure stuff."* Captain Sutter arrived at the camp the following day and inspected the millrace. He, too, found several pieces of gold, and begged all concerned to maintain secrecy for at least six weeks. Sutter reasoned once word got out, his nearly completed gristmill and sawmill projects would be abandoned before he could regain financial solvency and repay his debts. But the secret soon burned through the leather gold pouches and escaped.

It is possible the first to tell of the gold discovery were the Native American workers who communicated in their own language, within their own community, and didn't feel bound by any promise to Captain Sutter. The first white American to let the news slip might have been one of the "battalion boys" one night at the hotel or a store in Benicia. Even John Sutter, himself, could not contain his own secret, making an oblique reference to the discovery in conversation with his friend Mariano Vallejo. And Mrs. Wimmer confided in a teamster named Jacob Wittmer, making a delivery of supplies to the camp, who managed to find a few flecks as well. Wittmer then tried to purchase liquor from Brannan and Smith's general store with the gold dust and told C.C. Smith that Sutter could verify it being real. Sutter confirmed it to C.C. Smith. Smith told Brannan. And Sam Brannan would soon tell the world.

In order to secure legal title to the discovery site from military governor Richard Mason, Sutter sent another sawmill supervisor, Charles Bennett, to San Francisco on Feb. 8, 1848. Sutter had quickly "leased" the land from the local natives. However, the law was vague regarding what was federal land, public land or land protected under former Spanish and Mexican land grants and Governor Mason rejected Sutter's claim. Bennett showed samples of gold to several people including Brannan. Brannan had heard the rumor and had now seen the evidence. He quickly made his own way to Coloma and confirmed the discovery and immediately leased more space at Sutter's Fort and increased his inventory with every available pick, pan and shovel, anticipating the demand to come. As individuals caught wind of the news, those same individuals began trickling into the area around the Coloma site, where James Marshall continued to maintain the sawmill operation, thinking the discovery was small and limited. But Marshall's workers were gradually drifting off to do their own prospecting outside Sutter's claim. Soon traces of gold were being found all along the foothills of the Sierra Nevada, in veins that would extend north and south for over a hundred miles and become known as the Mother Lode. Even larger findings appeared at a downstream workcamp known as Mormon Island. Individuals became groups as most of the male population of northern California suspended their daily jobs or left their farms and headed for the hills. Sutter's nightmare came true as his employees walked away from the unfinished gristmill and left the hides in the tannery to rot. Eventually, even Suttter yielded to the lure of gold and moved into the gold fields with a small army of Native American and Kanaka (Hawaiian) workers.

By 1848, Sam Brannan was occupied with his enterprise at Sutter's Fort, glad to be away from the backbiting of his congregation and his running feuds with San Francisco elected officials. *The California Star* was returning him a steady income stream as publisher, and he had left the day-to-day editorial operation to Edward Kemble. Circulation was nearing 400 subscribers, greater than the literate population at the time. By the third edition of volume II, in January 1848, *The Star* had expanded to a larger four column sheet. Like most, Edward Kemble was convinced the future of California would be in agricultural development over time. Kemble was an able newspaperman, though still quite young, but his lack of real reporting experience caused him to at first miss the greatest scoop of his career and one of the biggest news stories of the century. Rumors of mineral wealth had circulated in California since Spanish times. Even when shown samples of gold in early March 1848, Kemble discounted the possibility, thinking the samples mica or pyrite – fool's gold. It would be almost another month before *The Star* casually mentioned that gold was being exchanged for goods at Sutter's Fort.

Still the rumors persisted, as rumors do. Kemble joined a party visiting the discovery site, only to find the workers there evasive as to the discovery of gold. Unable to elicit information from his interviewing the millworkers, nor finding any tangible evidence of gold at the site himself, Kemble stuck to his pastoral vision of California's future. He described talk of gold as *"humbug."* Thus, it was left to the competitor, *The Californian*, which had removed from Monterey the previous year to San Francisco to be closer to editor Semple's land development interests in the rival city of Benicia, to breathe the first public mention on March 15, 1848, *"that gold has been found in considerable quantities"*[5] at Sutter's mill. But few noticed the news item. Three days later, *The California Star* followed up by printing a general mining roundup story:

> *"We were informed a few days since, that a very valuable silver mine was situated above this place, and again, that its locality was known. Mines of quicksilver are being found all over the country. Gold has been discovered in the Northern Sacramento Districts, about forty miles above Sutter's Fort. Rich mines of copper are said to exist north of these bays."*[6]

Two weeks later, the *Star* reported:

> *"So great a quantity of gold taken from the mine recently found at New Helvetia, that it has become an article of the traffic in that vicinity."*[7]

But the story remained very much local news. The general public remained skeptical.

For several weeks, Sam Brannan, on behalf of the San Francisco merchant community, had been planning a pair of extra editions of the *California Star*, designed to showcase the wonders and opportunities awaiting newcomers to California. The publication would be designed to attract a wide readership in the United States, not specifically aimed at members of the Latter-Day Saints. This secular piece of 19th century public relations marked the first widescale effort to attract population migration by extolling the virtues of the future Golden State – a trend that has continued to modern times, whether touting orange groves, Hollywood, aerospace or high technology. Of course, Brannan's business enterprises would be a primary beneficiary of an influx of settlers.

To write the piece, Brannan contracted with Dr. Victor J. Fourgeaud, a transplanted South Carolinian, who had experienced firsthand much of north-central California and had a talent as a wordsmith. As Fourgeaud began his manuscript, the discovery of gold was still under wraps. His charge was to create awareness, stimulate interest and motivate action among potential immigrants, all classic communication techniques. At the same time, Fourgeaud was to counter negativity about California being spread by eastern and border states such as Missouri, suddenly concerned about a population drain with westward expansion. When the news of gold broke, coincidentally in the same special edition of *The Star,* on April 1st, those few sentences would outweigh the pages of Fourgeaud's florid prose.

Just as the labor-intensive typesetting of the dense, four column, six page extra must have taken weeks, so too would reading the published journal, devoid of white space, rules, illustrations, headlines or anything else that would break up the pages of type and enhance readability, be a chore. Once committed, the reader was presented with a virtual encyclopedia article about California:

> *"A cursory glance over the region known as 'Upper California' is sufficient to prove that no other country possesses a more varied soil, or one capable of producing in greater abundance all vegetable substances. Where will you find richer lands than those which border the Sacramento and San Joaquin? These can be drained at a comparatively small expense, and all the products belonging to a temperate climate may be furnished by this region alone."*[8]

The publication also contained two columns of current shipping news as well as the back page given over largely to advertising for hotels, merchandise ranging from window glass to furniture, lumber and all matter of commodities, and a pair of ads from C.C. Smith & Co., at New Helvetia:

> *C.C. SMITH CO.*
> *NEW HELVETIA*
>
> *HAVE JUST RECEIVED and offer for sale*
> *A New and General Assortment of*
> *Summer Clothing, Coats, Vests, and Pant*
> *Tsaloons, cheap for cash*
> *-also-*
> *Keep constantly on hand, the necessary*

Outfit for parties wishing to cross the mountains with pack animals – viz: Riding and Pack saddles, Par-fleshes, &c. &c.[9]

Because Fourgeaud wrote this piece in the early months of 1848, before the discovery of gold became public knowledge, and perhaps also because editor Kemble and even publisher Brannan remained skeptical about the existence of great wealth from the earth, there is scant attention paid to a discussion of minerology in the article – virtually nothing on the front page. However, by careful scanning of the entire edition, the astute copy editors of eastern newspapers could pick out nuggets of a golden story, sprinkled through the generic text like flakes in the streambed.

"California is well known to be rich in mineral wealth: – Iron, copper, lead, sulphur, silver, quicksilver, gold &c. are known to exist, and are believed to be abundant in quantity and rich in quality. Some of these mines are now in operation, and large amounts of capital will be invested in the business, and numerous laborers employed as soon as the necessary machinery can be obtained."[10]

On the second page:

"A Silver mine has been discovered in the neighborhood of the Pueblo, a Coppermine in Napa, and Gold at Sutter's. A man positively picked $30 worth of gold from the sand in one day. This I have from an undoubted source."[11]

And on page 3:

> *"And without allowing any golden hopes to puzzle my prophetic vision of the future, I would predict for California a Peruvian harvest of the precious metals, so soon as a sufficiency of miners, minerologists and metallogists find their way thither, and commence disimbouging her rich hidden treasures."*[12]

All these mentions are generalized accounts and perhaps wishful speculation. It wasn't until that paragraph buried on the fourth page, in the article about the Great Sacramento Valley, that Fourgeaud specifically mentions the gold strike at Sutter's mill as a statement of fact. And this small mention – almost as an aside – would catch the attention of the *New York Herald,* and the press of the world shortly thereafter.

As soon as the special edition came off the press, Brannan had 2,000 copies of the papers bundled and entrusted to ten men, hired as couriers to take the papers to cities in the Mississippi Valley, and then mailed farther east, including to New York and the National Library at Washington D.C. Individual copies were distributed to travelers encountered on the trail. Most of these messengers were Mormon Battalion veterans anxious to return to families somewhere between Council Bluff and Salt Lake, and happy to have Brannan's stipend to finance their journey. After arriving at Salt Lake, half the riders decided to remain there; the rest pushed on across the prairie. In the Black Hills, the couriers intercepted Brigham Young, leading his second band of settlers to the Salt Lake Valley. When Young heard of the potential gold of California, the Mormon Moses doubled down on his vow not to settle on the Pacific coast, where gold would compete for his people's worship. Ironically, the express riders had shown Young gold they, themselves, had found at Mormon's Island. By mid-summer, the post riders had delivered their newspapers and the national press was soon on alert.

The *New York Herald* did make note of the California news by August, though many newspapers regarded the rumors as unfounded hyperbole and refused to cover the story. By September, the *Herald* was like a dog with a bone, reprinting letters from a correspondent, known as Paisano, describing gold discoveries in California. At the same time, private correspondence from California began to arrive by post in eastern America and some newspapers began reprinting those letters. Gradually, news from California was knocking from the front-page national coverage of the upcoming presidential election between the Whigs Party candidate, General Zachary Taylor and a divided Democratic Party split between Lewis Cass and former president Martin van Buren. Even the galvanizing issue of slavery and the possibility of California entering the union as a slave state was not sufficient to dominate the news.

The news crossed the Atlantic via steamship by October, and the venerable *Times* of London picked up the story, although it advised its readers to exercise caution in reading of the gold discovery. The story migrated to the continent, but Europe, caught up in another revolution in France, cholera epidemics and other conflicts and civil wars, relegated the story to the back pages as filler.

Meanwhile, in the United States, news of the gold strike had filtered into the pages of big city dailies in New York, Philadelphia, Baltimore, St. Louis and New Orleans among others. And increasingly it occupied part of the national conversation. Official communication from U.S. Navy agent Thomas Larkin, Commodore Thomas ap Catsby Jones and Governor Richard Mason dispelled much lingering doubt. Samples of gold had been sent to Washington D.C. by special messenger. Any residual doubts were swept away by President James K. Polk's confirmation of the discovery in his State of the Union Address on Dec. 5th. Let the Gold Rush begin!

No longer engaged enough to tolerate the petty squabbles of his flock, Samuel Brannan had delivered what would be his final sermon to his Mormon followers on April 30, 1848. He next sailed to Benicia and took a horse on to Sutter's Fort before visiting the "gold mine" on Mormon's Island. There he became convinced of the magnitude of the gold strike and the opportunities it presented. Brannan had also tried to secure title to gold country land but was unsuccessful as had been Sutter. Governor Mason felt granting land was a congressional prerogative, rather than that of the governor. Governor Mason had visited Mormon Island in July 1848, accompanied by his military aide Lieutenant William T. Sherman, who later recalled the visit:

> *"As soon as the fame of the gold discovery spread through California, the Mormons naturally turned to Mormon Island...Sam Brannan was on hand, as the high priest, collecting the tithes...*

> *"I remember that Mr. Clark* [one of several Clarks, including Mormon Battalion veterans] *was in camp, talking to Colonel Mason about matters and things generally, when he inquired,* "Governor, what business has Sam Brannan to collect the tithes

here?'...Colonel Mason answered, 'Brannan has a perfect right to collect the tax, if you Mormons are fools enough to pay it.' I understood, afterward, that from that time the payment of tithes ceased, but Brannan had already collected enough money wherewith to hire Sutter's hospital, and to open a store there, in which he made more money than any merchant in California during that summer and fall."[13]

In fact, the money (or gold equivalent) that Brannan had been collecting was not a 10 percent tithe; rather it was a 30 percent finder's fee divided among battalion veterans Sidney Willes and Wilford Hudson who had found the gold at Mormon Island, and Sam Brannan who nominally was securing title to the strike. It was all payable to Sam Brannan & Co. Not all the miners paid the fee and it abruptly ended following the governor's visit. But by then, Brannan was back at his Sutter's Fort business, investing the funds in his enterprise. Addison Pratt, president of the San Francisco branch of the Church wrote:

This place [Mormon Island] had been discovered by two men of the Mormon Battalion by the names of Willis and Hudson. When we arrived there, we found that Brannan had entered into a league with them, to make all that dug there pay them thirty percent of all they should find there. The pretence [sic] was, that they were intending to help the church with this percentage by buying young cattle in California and sending them to Salt Lake. I had seen enough of Brannan's tricks to convince me that the church would never see any cattle brought to them through that channel.[14]

Brannan was anxious to generate business over the discovery of gold. He collected samples of the precious golden metal in a quinine bottle and hurried back to San Francisco. In an account by early California historian H.H. Bancroft that may be partially apocryphal, on May 10, Brannan reportedly stepped from the ferry, swinging his hat in one hand and the vial of gold dust in the other, crying, *"Gold! Gold! Gold from the American River."*[15] His cry raced through San Francisco like electricity. Within hours, would-be gold seekers began to leave the city; within weeks the city was nearly empty. Before leaving San Francisco with another boat load of merchandise for his store, Brannan advised a group of Saints to go off to the mines. He would never meet with his Mormons again.

In the excitement of Brannan's public announcement, editor Kemble continued to hold a skeptical view. Unable to confirm the rumors now swirling through the entire region, Kemble likened himself to Don Quixote, charging at windmills (This may have been a clever double entendre: the competition newspaper, *Californian*, was now housed in an old adobe at the base of a giant windmill.) It was Edward Kemble who named the phenomenon *"gold fever."* Some later historians, in trying to disparage Brannan, argued that the publisher pressured Kemble to embargo news of gold long enough for Brannan to better position his mercantile enterprise for the coming business bonanza. Evidence, however, suggests young Kemble was simply cautious in the extreme – until it was out of his control.

On May 29th, the rival newspaper *Californian,* in the midst of management changes, closed its doors with the following message:

> *"We have also received information that very many of our subscribers in various parts of the country have left their usual places of abode and gone to the gold region, showing that this fever (to which the cholera is a mere bungler in the way of depopulating towns) is not confined to San Francisco alone....The whole country, from San Francisco to Los Angeles, and from the sea shore to the base of the Sierra Nevadas, resounds with the cry of 'gold, GOLD, **GOLD**."*[16]

At *The California Star,* Kemble appealed to his readers' reason about believing tales of golden rivers and he encouraged them to pay their subscriptions before leaving for the gold fields. Kemble also promised his readers an update on the gold story in the next edition, which reversed the conclusions of all his previous reporting. But it was too late. Kemble's printer, a man named T.H. Rolfe and the compositor called Yates had both defected to the gold fields. Within two weeks, *The Star* also capitulated and followed its competition into hiatus, if not oblivion. In a tersely worded statement, Kemble announced on June 14th:

> *"We appear before the remnant of a reading community with the material or immaterial information that we have stopped the paper – that its publication ceased with the last regular issue."*[17]

Promising to revive the publication in an enhanced format in the future, Kemble bid his readers *"Hasta luego!"* and locked the doors before heading to the gold fields himself.

San Francisco was briefly without a newspaper. But it would become a newspaper town once again. Sam Brannan's *The California Star* would be resurrected under a new name with Edward C. Kemble back as both editor and publisher, solidifying his reputation as the premier journalist of his day. Nevertheless, for the rest of his career, Kemble would second-guess himself over his handling of the biggest news story of the first half of the 19th century, that of the discovery of gold in California. As for publisher Samuel Brannan, he had not only started the city's newspaper tradition, but he had also officially given San Francisco its name and played the role of Herald to the Gold Rush. He would yet do even more.

Notes

1. Jefferson Hunt, letter to Brigham Young, May 14, 1847, Brigham Young Collection, LDS Archives.

2. Samuel Brannan, letter to Brigham Young, October 17, 1847, Journal History, LDS Archives.

3. James W. Marshall, "Marshall's Own Account of the Gold Discovery," *The Century Illustrated* Monthly Magazine, February 1891.

4. Ibid.

5. *The Californian*, March 15, 1848.

6. *The California Star,* March 18, 1848.

7. Ibid., March 25, 1848.

8. Ibid., April 1, 1848.

9. Ibid.

10. Ibid.

11. Ibid.

12. Ibid.

13. William Tecumseh Sherman, Memoirs of General William T. Sherman by Himself, pp. 52-53.

14. S. George Ellsworth ed., The Journals of Addison Pratt, Salt Lake City: university of Utah Press, 1990, pp. 336-337.

15. H. Bancroft, History of California, The History Co. 1886-1890, p. 56.

16. *The Californian*, May 29, 1848.

17. *The California Star*, June 14, 1848.

Chapter 9
The Emporium of the Pacific

"Cities are like gentlemen, they are born not made... I bet San Francisco was a city from the very first time it had a dozen settlers."

– Will Rogers

"This Street is impassable. Not even Jackassable."

– Sign on the corner of Clay and Kearny Streets, warning of muddy conditions that could swallow man or beast, Winter 1849

For most of 1848, the California Gold Rush was a local affair. The first to try their luck at finding gold had been the very mill workers and indigenous First Peoples employed at Sutter's Mill. And they proved lucky indeed. Many found gold by simply looking down into stream beds or picking visible pieces out of the hillside with the points of their Bowie knives. They were quickly followed by other locals up from Sutter's Fort, the surrounding *ranchos* and soon from San Francisco.

The next wave was regional. Because communication was dependent on transportation, news of the gold strike was next carried to Pacific ports in Oregon, southern California, Mexico and the Sandwich Islands by steamships. From there, the ships sailed on to ports as far away as Peru and Chile, or even China or Australia. And soon gold seekers began coming to California from all these places. Meanwhile, the news had barely trickled back east into the United States, where it received a skeptical reception. By the time gold fever-infected Americans made either the long trip across North America and over the Sierra, the longer trip by ship around Cape Horn or the shorter, quicker, more expensive route crossing the Isthmus of Panama, much of the easy pickings had already been found. The great deluge of people began in 1849, and they became known as Forty Niners. They came by the thousands, and then tens of thousands and finally perhaps a quarter million came from all over the world – a global migration never before witnessed.

While prospecting proved to require as much luck as skill, it always required hard work. Miners spent hours in icy streams, bent over with picks and shovels, attacking rocky hillsides and moving acres of mud and sand, searching for a few bright, shiny flakes of gold. Living conditions were often unhealthy, violent and brutally primitive. Sanitation was non-existent. Even the most essential supplies were of limited availability and very expensive. Some miners found enough to cover their expenses or even a small profit. A smaller number made their fortunes. But many others found nothing but disappointment. Like any addiction, gold mining offered the promise of striking it rich at the next diggings, the next hill or stream – or maybe the ones after that.

By the end of 1848, ships of every type, from all nations, began to funnel through the golden gateway and clog the harbor of San Francisco, as the city became the jumping-off point for prospectors heading to the gold fields. Many of the original inhabitants of San Francisco who had rushed to the hills at the first whisper of gold, returned with enough gold dust in their poke to re-start their abandoned businesses or start new ones. Almost overnight, San Francisco bounced back from ghost town to boom town, as the population swelled with each arriving vessel in the port, disgorging legions of new hopefuls. Entire ships' crews deserted their vessels and headed for the mines. Many ships were abandoned, though some became repurposed for use on the bay, as warehouses, or even as the local jail. Other ships were simply left to rot and used as bay-fill. Cargoes of every description were gobbled up and resold at grossly inflated prices to a consuming public that couldn't get enough of everything. Money flowed through San Francisco like the Sacramento River at flood stage and gold dust was the common currency. Employment was universal and wages were high. Land speculators made vast profits. Banks flourished to safeguard the gold deposits; dens of all manner of vice sprung up to relieve the miners of their treasure before it ever got to the bank.

As hundreds of ships crowded with thousands of argonauts and tons of heavy freight made their way from eastern ports like New York or Baltimore and sailed for months via Drake's Passage around the tip of Cape Horn and thence up the west coast of South and Central America to San Francisco, others hurried to the gold by crossing the Isthmus of Panama, cutting months off the journey. In 1848, Congress authorized establishment of two steamship companies to transport mail between New York and San Francisco: the U.S. Mail Steam Line on the Atlantic, with ports in Charleston, Savannah, New Orleans, Havana and Chagres, and on the Pacific coast the

Pacific Mail Steamship Company sailing between Panama City and Monterey, San Francisco and Astoria, Oregon. The 60-mile, week-long journey across the Isthmus entailed a 20-mile mule train ride through virgin jungle and mangrove swamps, followed by negotiating the alligator-filled Chagres River and clouds of sand flies and mosquitoes in a dugout canoe called a *bungo.* (A narrow-gauge railroad would be completed by the mid-1850s, shortening the crossing from days to hours and increasing the comfort and safety.) With completion of the Panama rail line, faster ships and better coordination between Atlantic and Pacific sailing schedules, the entire journey could be completed in less than a month; the fastest sailing ships sailing around Cape Horn made the trip in three months. During the gold rush, these shipping companies played a key role in moving goods, mail and passengers, thereby developing San Francisco into the major commercial hub of the Pacific coast.

The Gold Rush created an enormous economic stimulus for the United States. Gold would help retire the Mexican War debt. Eastern manufacturing and southern agriculture thrived on meeting the enhanced demand. Migration to the gold fields absorbed thousands of otherwise unemployed Mexican War veterans and avoided a national recession. By early spring 1849, Midwesterners began snaking long wagon trains across the continent, following the same overland route the Mormons had used before turning toward the Salt Lake Valley. Timing was crucial. These emigrants –almost entirely men – had to wait until spring grass had grown along the prairie route to provide fodder for their oxen or horses, yet, mindful of the fate of the Donner Party, they needed to reach the Sierra Nevada mountains before the winter snows. That timetable also placed them in the Great Basin Desert at high summer. Scarcity of food, fuel, and safe drinking water, combined with heat, drought, torrential floods, swarms of insects, cholera outbreaks and hostile Native Americans, plagued these Forty Niners each mile of the three-to-six-month journey. The California Trail became littered with discarded possessions, broken wagons, the carcasses of dead animals and other evidence of dashed dreams. By the time these hearty gold-seekers crossed the Sierra passes and reached the foothill gold camps and valleys below, they had endured such hardship that only the lure of gold had kept their wagons rolling west.

Not all Gold Rush fortunes came out of a shallow miner's pan. Supplying the miners and mining camps with everything from food, tools and hardware to entertainment in makeshift saloons, gambling dens and brothels often yielded the proprietors large rewards and left the miners to try and scratch out some more yellow dust from the earth. Some of these entrepreneurs became wealthy in the process. Garment manufacturer Levi Strauss operated several dry goods shops in San Francisco, selling clothing, blankets and duck cloth for tenting and wagon tops. (He would one day join with a Reno tailor named Jacob Davis to manufacture denim workpants, reinforced with metal rivets, still being made and known worldwide as Levis.) Dry goods merchant and wholesale grocer Leland Stanford ran a general merchandise store in Michigan Bluff in Placer County, serving the needs of the miners. Stanford would go on to partner in the transcontinental railroad, serve as California governor and senator, and found a university named for his son. At Sutter's Fort, Sam Brannan bought out his partner C.C. Smith for some $50,000 and renamed the store S. Brannan & Co. He opened other stores in Coloma and Mormon Island, thus dominating the gold country market. He bought up all available mining supplies and other merchandise in San Francisco and within three weeks sold out at such inflated prices that he is often acknowledged as California's first millionaire.

While others made fortunes, for Captain John Sutter the gold discovery proved calamitous. His own foray into the gold country floundered when he was unable to coerce the Native Nisenan Indians to do his mining in the American River watershed. Lacking the business acumen of Brannan, Sutter's own attempts at mercantilism also failed. In 1849, nearly 80,000 immigrants to California passed by Sutter's Fort. His empire was based on land and that land was increasingly overrun by these gold seeking immigrants who culled Sutter's herds for food and his fields for forage for their own animals. Unable to evict the squatters, Sutter became increasingly despondent and turned more often to the bottle for solace.

In Switzerland, Sutter's estranged wife, Anna, read reports of the California Gold Rush and after 15 years learned the whereabouts of her husband. Mrs. Sutter and their now-grown son John Augustus Jr., called August, made their way to North America and reunited with the captain. In an attempt to escape his mounting debts, Sutter transferred title to his remaining holdings to his son before selling the fort for $7,000 and taking his family north to their Hock Farm near Marysville. The ever-persuasive Sam Brannan convinced Sutter Jr. into a partnership to use Sutter's assets in the development of a new city at the confluence of the American and Sacramento Rivers. It would be called Sacramento.

Unlike Sutter, Brannan used his newfound fortune to generate even more wealth. Shuttling between San Francisco and his properties on the Sacramento River, Brannan invested heavily in San Francisco real estate, underwrote civic projects, supported public charities and wielded political influence as one of the first elected San Francisco city councilors. At Sacramento, Brannan and his partners laid out a township along the waterfront, called the Embarcadero, and began regular shipping in San Francisco Bay. With partner John Fowler, an overland Mormon pioneer whose wife, Jerusha, had been a passenger on the *Brooklyn*, they used lumber from Sutter's mill to build an elegant hotel along the quayside which became immediately profitable. Many other investors and merchants followed Brannan in the development of the new city, despite Sutter's warnings that the area was flood prone. A relatively dry winter of 1849 lulled the entrepreneurs into a false sense of security. In future years, Old Sacramento would flood severely, and the foundations of buildings would eventually be raised several feet to escape the rising waters. (Sutter, himself, had attempted to develop a community farther south, on higher ground, but it, too, was an unsuccessful venture.)[1.] In 1854, the state legislature relocated to Sacramento and at the 1879 state constitutional convention, Sacramento was named permanent state capital.

R.F. Peckham would recall the evolution of Sacramento in an article in the *San Jose Pioneer* in 1877:

> *"The most of what is known as Sacramento City, was then a dense swamp. Wise gentlemen* [John

Sutter and Lansford Hastings], *in the Fall of that year* [1848], *surveyed and mapped out a town on the high land, three miles below* [Sutter's Fort] *and called it Sutterville, and here is where the city should have been built. But Samuel Brannan decreed otherwise, and the low swamp at the junction of the Sacramento and American rivers was made the commercial emporium of the valley and the Sierras."*[2]

Preoccupied with his business interests, Sam Brannan no longer involved himself in the activities of his church. He had not heard from the church leadership in more than a year, not since his supplication of loyalty to Brigham Young. Brannan took the marginalization as a personal insult, and he felt betrayed. Although Brigham Young had repeatedly warned against the lure of gold and discouraged his followers from heading to California, he nevertheless understood the powerful effect an infusion of gold would have upon the success of his Salt Lake ambitions. The first wagon load of gold from California arrived at Salt Lake in September 1848. As late as Spring 1849, Young continued to insist that the Saints remain in Salt Lake and devote their efforts to agriculture rather than go gold mining. But gradually, Young's pragmatic side dictated that California gold was an important source of much needed capital and he surreptitiously authorized groups of "missionaries" to return to California to quietly mine for gold. Salt Lake also profited from the Gold Rush by providing food, rest and supplies for thousands of immigrants heading to California, and by the end of 1848, Young had established a mint at Salt Lake, converting at a commission gold nuggets and dust into coin. The early success of the Salt Lake venture was due, in large part, to California gold.

It seems the Mormon hierarchy would have been pleased to wash its hands of Samuel Brannan, but it could not ignore his vast fortune nor his political influence in California. Missionary Wilford Woodruff, staying in the Boston home of Brannan's sister, Mary Ann Badlam, wrote to Brannan in September 1848, requesting Brannan to reply with a check anywhere from 25 cents to $25,000 from his gold diggings [for the Church, implied].

In March 1849, Brannan corresponded with his sister, tellingly revealing the depth of his feelings toward the Mormon leadership: (Brannan was a notoriously poor speller and writer.):

> *"Any news you may have from this Country as a Golden one you Can Believe for you have not heard half the truth. With in the Last year I have Cleared over a Hundred Thousand Dollars and hope to* [keep] *This from the authorities of the Church. They have forsaken me. I Have Been Here three years and over and Received No account only What I traveled Clear to the Salt Lake after. No one Ever thought Enough of Me During my Long Stay here to Wright to Me and in fact I am unable to See What I Was Sent here for unless it Was to Get me out of the Way Supposing it Being a Spanish Country i Would Be Killed* [sic]*."*[3]

A copy of Brannan's letter was forwarded to Brigham Young who at last replied to Brannan in April 1849. In his impersonal letter, Young entreated Brannan to remit what he considered owed. At the time, the Mormon leadership relied entirely on church funds for their livelihood and the Church stood impoverished. In asking Brannan for some $50,000 to be divided between Young and his two senior counselors, the Mormon leader saw no conflict of interest in using church monies for his personal expenses. Young appealed to Brannan's faith as well as his acquisitiveness with the argument that the more Brannan gave, the more the Lord would allow him to get. It is unclear whether Brigham Young ever expected Brannan to honor the request. There is no mention of Brannan's continuing role in the Church:

> *"...If you want to continue to prosper do not forget the Lord's Treasury, lest he forget you, and with the liberal, the Lord is liberal; and when you have settled with the treasury, I want you to remember, that, Bro Brigham has long been destitute of a home, and suffered heavy loses & incurred great expenses in searching out a location and planting a church in this place, & he wants you to send him a present of twenty thousand dollars in gold dust to help him in his labors. This is but a trifle, when gold is so plenty, but it will do me much good at this time.* "[4]

The nature of Brannan's use of Saints' tithings had dogged him since the very arrival of the *Brooklyn* at Yerba Buena, through his colony at New Hope, the various investments of S. Brannan & Co., and the misconstrued management fee at Mormon Island. From this arose the most famous of Brannan legends: that he claimed he would remit the

Lord's money to Brigham Young when the Lord provided a signed receipt. The story is likely grounded in some fact; Brannan may have said something to that effect, or it may have originated from John Sutter. Brannan would retell it many times in later years, embellishing it with each glass of alcohol and relishing the memory of outwitting Brigham Young. But as each historian and biographer recast it, it became embedded in Brannan lore. At the time of the Gold Rush, Brannan did repay the Church some minor outstanding debts. To his mind, he had cleared the books and severed any remaining financial obligations to the Church. Contrary to beliefs then and now, when Brannan was ultimately disassociated from the Church of Jesus Christ of Latter-Day Saints, it would not be for any embezzlement or misuse of church funds.

In San Francisco, Brannan headed a project to build a long wharf far into the Bay to accommodate the largest ocean-going ships. He built a large home for his family on the corner of Stockton and Washington Streets and entertained lavishly. He cultivated the patronage of the elite of California government, business and society, and they cultivated him. In Gold Rush California, San Francisco was the most important city and Samuel Brannan was its most successful, most important son.

San Francisco did not remain without its newspapers for long. The first to return from hiatus, as promised, was the *Californian* in July 1848, under direction of printer B.F. Foster. It published on an irregular schedule without permanent management until mid-November when it breathed its last as an independent newspaper and merged with its former rival, *The California Star*.

In late September, *The Star's* former editor E.C. Kemble abandoned his attempts at gold mining and returned to what he knew best. He approached Sam Brannan, who still owned the publication, with a purchase offer. *The Star* had been profitable from its first edition, but in Brannan's world, everything was for sale. Brannan was moving on to enterprises of a grander scale and accepted Kemble's $800 offer. Kemble next proposed a partnership with the *Californian*, whose debt-ridden publishers gladly agreed to the merger and then promptly skipped town on a ship to the Sandwich Islands, leaving Kemble alone to face the creditors. Kemble skillfully found a printer, combined the subscriber lists of both newspapers and cobbled together enough advertising and job printing revenue to publish the joint *Star and Californian* through the rest of the year. In December, Kemble announced a change, as he recalled in his 1858 *History of California Newspapers*:

> *"The next number announces the close of the publication under the joint names of the old papers, and a new arrangement, new journal, new name and new partners, more suited to the altered circumstances of the country, to begin with the new year. The same paper contains the first notice of the 'new town of Sacramento.' But the most cheering signs of progress which were set in the sky when the old pioneer journals of the Territory were laid in the grave – the most hopeful rays which illuminated their closing pages...were the signal fires of the approaching political revolution, the beacon lights in the path of the new State."*[5]

Aware that publishing a newspaper in Gold Rush San Francisco was beyond the capacity of a single individual, Kemble enlisted another printing associate named Edward Gilbert as a partner in the new venture. Gilbert had served as an officer in the New York Volunteers during the Mexican War and agreed to the partnership, assuming half the outstanding debt (A problematic third partner was subsequently added.) On January 4, 1849, California's two original newspapers, the *Californian* and *The California Star* were reincarnated as the *Alta California*. The "*Alta*" would chronicle the events of California for the rest of the 19th century and employ some of America's most renowned journalists and writers, most famously Mark Twain. But its predecessors had paved the way, building a new city and opening golden California to the world.

Notes

1. California began recording rainfall and snowpack in 1849. As this is being written, after several years of drought, California has experienced a near-record rainy winter and record snow fall in the Sierra. Several communities statewide have experienced flooding. Record windstorms have toppled thousands of trees. A warm spring and early thaw could seriously challenge the integrity of the vast system of levees now protecting cities and agricultural land in the Sacramento Valley. While drought, wildfire and flood cycles have always been the pattern of California's environment, current climate change seems to be intensifying the effects and the frequency.

2. R.F. Peckham, "An Eventful Life," *San Jose Pioneer,* July 14, 1877 pp. 6-7.

3. Samuel Brannan, Letter to Mary Ann and Alexander Badlam, March 13, 1849.

4. Brigham Young, Letter to Samuel Brannan, April 5, 1849.

5. Edward C. Kemble and Helen Harding Bretnor (ed.), <u>A History of California Newspapers, 1846 – 1858</u>, Los Gatos, CA: The Talisman Press, 1962, pp. 87-88. Kemble refers to the Territory. In fact, California was never a U.S. Territory but was fast-tracked into statehood in 1850.

Epilogue

"East is east, and west is San Francisco."

– O. Henry

"The gold rush has never stopped: The new Argonauts are just looking for a different El Dorado"

– Gary Kamiya,
"Requiems for a Dream,"
The End of the Golden Gate, 2021

B y late 1849-1850, the "Eureka" moments of the Gold Rush had passed. The easiest pickings which produced easy fortunes had already dried up. The Sierra foothills had been explored and exploited from one end to the other. Pick and pan mining had started to be replaced by industrial scale hydraulic mining, blasting less accessible mountainsides with water cannon. The numbers of disappointed and discouraged Forty Niners abandoning the gold fields and leaving California began to exceed the inflow of new hopefuls. But many others stayed in the west, claiming the best farmland and swelling the population of San Francisco and the even newer Sacramento. (At this writing, some 174 years after the Gold Rush, the unusually heavy California winter rains and snowpack melt have dislodged rocky hillsides and scoured mountain streams, exposing new deposits of gold, to the delight of amateur prospectors and weekend mining hobbyists.)

In order to accommodate a population surging to more than 30,000, San Francisco had to expand beyond its Gold Rush boundaries. San Francisco became a legally incorporated city with the adoption of a charter in 1850. The following year, the newly created U.S.-style city government annexed the unsurveyed sand dunes west of Larkin Street. Soon the giant "Steam Paddy" steam shovel, so-called because it replaced scores of Irish workers, was plowing into sand dunes as high as 200 feet and leveling this Western Addition to be surveyed, subdivided and auctioned off by the city for revenue. The older sections of the city became more cosmopolitan, with hotels, fine restaurants, masonry construction, wooden sidewalks and sewers. Yet most of the city was still constructed of canvas and wood and open fires provided the only heat and light. San Francisco would suffer five devastating fires during this period, resulting in enormous financial loss. Mercenary entrepreneurs charged money to help fight fires and threatened arson when the city denied their claims. Ships of the world anchored at San Francisco and steamers regularly plied the bay and upstream to Sacramento. Almost overnight, The City grew from youth to maturity, skipping an adolescence. But with the maturity, wealth and sophistication came a darker side: vice, crime and corruption.

Of all the entrepreneurs, hustlers, swindlers and gamblers in San Francisco, **Sam Brannan** was the most astute, nimble and lucky. His business speculations, often risky, thrived in the chaotic climate of the later Gold Rush years. Not even staggering financial loss from a pair of devastating fires set him back. He invested widely, donated generously, advocated vigorously and maintained a hedonistic lifestyle to match his appetite for business. It was to protect these business interests that led Brannan to an episode in his career that would rupture his relationship with the Church for good.

Following the California legislature's Foreign Miners Tax in 1850, most non-Americans left the gold fields. Many were absorbed into San Francisco. Chinese and Latin Americans made up almost half the population and many Australians had been deported from British debtors' prisons to California. They all lived in tents, crude wooden shanties or on board the abandoned ships in the bay. Given the complexion of the population and the wealth and alcohol flowing through San Francisco, it is not surprising that violent crime found its way to the city by the bay. But San Francisco was still nothing like lethal Five Points in New York City or lawless Tombstone, Arizona in later years. Nevertheless, merchants feared the various gangs that formed in the different neighborhoods and looked to Brannan as a natural leader to do something about them. Brannan had perhaps more to lose from gang violence and the threat of arson than most, and he was instrumental in founding the first "popular tribunal" to mete out vigilante justice in 1851. The first would-be victims were members of a gang called "Sydney Ducks," dockside Australians accused of robbery and assault. With Brannan at the head, a lynch mob urged city police to hang the suspects. Frustrated when the local authorities turned the mob away, the men organized a Committee of Vigilance to rid the city of crime. (The suspects were subsequently found to be innocent). The next suspect was in fact guilty, a robber caught after stealing a merchant's safe from an office on the long wharf. After a kangaroo court, the accused was taken to Portsmouth Square in the middle of the night and lynched from a beam of the Old Adobe. The *Alta* reported the incident:

> *"About 12 o'clock it was reported that he had been convicted and sentenced to be executed upon the Plaza. This statement was corroborated about an hour afterwards by Mr. Samuel Brannan, who addressed the populace, and informed them that the man had been fairly tried by a committee of citizens and that no doubt of his guilt existed...the rope was placed about his neck by a dozen willing hands, and he was immediately run up, struggling furiously...As we close this article the cor[p]se of the domed man is swinging in the night air, surrounded by a guard of the committee of citizens."* [1]

While several men admitted to having participated in the hanging, no individual accepted responsibility. No indictments were issued. The committee doubled in size, drank heavily and argued about how to be legitimate keepers of the peace. It kept up a regular schedule of fire patrols and administered punishments including whippings and deportations of the accused. On August 19th, Brannan and others arrested a pair of suspected murderers. A divided Vigilance Committee turned the suspects over to the police, but subsequently sprung the prisoners out of jail and summarily hung the pair as thousands watched. Brannan justified the action by claiming the men had confessed.

Shortly thereafter, Governor John MacDougal denounced the *"demonic control"* of the vigilantes and local military commander William Tecumseh Sherman threatened to intervene. The Committee seems to have spent its anger and it suspended further activity. Brannan tried to distance himself from all the group's actions. While Brannan and the vigilantes proved popular with many locals and were later remembered as wresting control of San Francisco from criminal gangs, many others objected to the Committee's motives and methods. There were those who would not overlook his role in the days of terror.

With the influx of so many thousands of Forty-Niners, the demographic dominance of Mormons in California dissipated and their influence waned. No Mormons would serve as delegates to the California Constitutional Convention. Many Saints made the reverse migration back to Utah while others drifted and were absorbed into the general gentile population. With the realization that the Church would receive no more funds from Samuel Brannan, the leadership decided it was time to sever its relationship with the errant Californian. Brannan had been a maverick leader from the early years, backing William Smith instead of Brigham Young as leader after Prophet Joseph Smith's murder; excommunicating members of the *Brooklyn* assembly with questionable authority; using – or misusing – members' tithings for personal gain; and publicly challenging Brigham Young over settling at Salt Lake. Brannan's earlier signing of the agreement with A.G. Benson & Co. to yield half of any Mormon-occupied territory to the government was a particularly galling irritant to Brigham Young, who demanded complete obedience. Some questioned whether Brannan had ever been a true believer. But his service to the Church as a publisher, an evangelist in New York and a skillful organizer of the exodus to California and establishment of a colony that flourished at Yerba Buena were all undeniable. However, even if his worldly pursuit of wealth, women, liquor and gambling could be overlooked, his association with the vigilante movement proved too much, and provided the rationale for disfellowship. Brannan was charged with apostasy, the willful renunciation of his beliefs. Brannan was separated from the Church by unanimous vote on August 25, 1851, for unchristian conduct, neglect of duties and joining in lawless illegal behavior leading to murder.[2] The disfellowship was administered by Elder Parley Pratt, who publicly regretted having endorsed Brannan years earlier. For his part, Brannan, freed from any restraints of church membership, remained openly critical of the Church, particularly the leadership of Brigham Young. Still, Brannan adhered to a personal theology closely tied to the earliest teachings of Joseph Smith and he maintained cordial and generous relationships with many individual Mormons for the rest of his life.

With the Compromise of 1850, Congress established the Territory of Utah, without deciding on its future status as a slave or free state. **Brigham Young** was appointed the first governor of the new territory. He oversaw the establishment of settlements in the future states of Utah, Idaho, California, Nevada, Arizona and Colorado, as well as in northern Mexico, and he spent huge sums on the development of their infrastructure. When efforts to merge California and Utah into a super-state were mounted, he argued instead for an independent State of Deseret, and the proposal died. He established schools and the college that would become Brigham Young University. Militantly defensive of his church, Young established a militia to protect its sovereignty. An autocrat by personality and practice, Young was controversial. He supported the expansion of slavery into Utah Territory. His advocacy of polygamy – he personally accounted for 56 wives, though not all in physical relationships – ignited the so-called "Utah War" of 1857-1858, put down by the incursion of 2,500 federal troops. Historians still debate the nature of any role he may have played in the 1857 Mountain Meadows Massacre, where 120 immigrants from Arkansas were systematically killed and their youngest children taken into Mormon families. Young opposed involvement in the Civil War and maintained church law superseded federal law. When he died from a ruptured appendix in 1870, he had served as President of the Church for 30 years and was the wealthiest man in Utah. For decades, the United States Congress had rejected Utah's bid for statehood fearing a theocracy in the new state and focusing its argument on the illegal practice of polygamy. The Church, bending to the will of the nation, renounced polygamy in 1890 and Utah was admitted to statehood in 1896.

In the post-Gold Rush era, Mormonism experienced periods of expansion and contraction in the Golden State. Brigham Youngs's earlier policy of practicing the religion quietly was reversed and public evangelism and missionary work accelerated. Dissension roiled the California Mormons over polygamy and slavery, just as those issues inflamed the general population. Although California became the launching place for missionaries heading into the Pacific, Young eventually called for Saints in California to reunite at their true spiritual home in the shadows of the Wasatch Mountains in Utah and many, though not all, California Mormons heeded the call. Brigham Young never forgave Brannan's affront to his authority and never changed his antipathy toward California, where he claimed hell reigned. To his followers, Brigham

Young was the inspired prophet who saved and delivered their religion. To others he seemed an undemocratic tyrant. To all, he was a force of nature.

The Americanization of California and the events surrounding the Gold Rush altered the life arc of all involved. **Guadalupe Mariano Vallejo** retired to his Rancho Petaluma Adobe and managed his 44,000-acre estate. He spent his energy persuading other wealthy *Californios* to accept the new reality of American administration and he served as a delegate to the State Constitutional Convention. In 1851, Vallejo donated 150 acres to establish a new California capital city, called Vallejo, when lawmakers rejected the first capital at San Jose after only a year. Although the Treaty of Guadalupe Hidalgo guaranteed the legality of former Mexican land grants, Vallejo drained his fortune defending his property in American courts and eventually lost most of his land to settle his legal fees. He lived on modestly and died in 1890, aged 83, at Sonoma, the city he had founded.

Despite eventual acquittal, **John Fremont** endured the humiliation of a court martial trial for mutiny, followed by the further humiliation of conviction of the lesser charges of disobedience to a superior officer and military misconduct. Although President James Polk commuted his dishonorable discharge, Fremont resigned from the Army and retreated to California. He had acquired the *rancho* of former governor Juan Bautista Alvarado called *Las Mariposas*, near Yosemite, and a gold strike at the *rancho* made Fremont a very wealthy man. Fremont would lead two more explorations of the west, scouting out possible transcontinental railroad routes. He was elected one of California's first U.S. senators as a Free-Soil

Democrat, though his opposition to slavery denied him a second term. In 1856, Fremont was nominated for the presidency by the newly organized Republican Party, but lost to the better funded Democrats behind James Buchanan, in a bitter election in which Fremont failed to carry his own state of California. Returning to the army as a major general at the start of the Civil War, Fremont was made commander of the Department of the West. His appointment of Ulysses S. Grant to split the Confederacy by controlling the Mississippi River would prove instrumental in winning the war, but his preemptive order to emancipate enslaved African Americans in Missouri proved too radical and he was removed from command by President Lincoln. After flirting with another presidential run with the Radical Democratic Party in 1864, the Fremonts retired to Sleepy Hollow, New York. He would later be appointed Governor of Arizona Territory, but he resigned rather than relocate to the southwest. John Fremont died unexpectedly of peritonitis in New York in 1890. Historians have long puzzled over how someone as brilliant as the "Pathfinder" could also manage to derail his own career so often. Nevertheless, Fremont's name is memorialized by countless counties, cities, schools, geographic features and other testimony to the would-be "Conqueror of California."

John Sutter emerged from retirement in the Fall of 1849 to serve as a delegate to the California Constitutional Convention. He was chosen to present the finished work to Governor Bennett Riley and called it the happiest day of his life. In 1853, the California State Legislature named Sutter major general in the state militia, giving the self-styled "Captain" the military commission he had long appropriated for himself. He and his wife lived at their Hock Farm on the Feather River until it burned in 1865. The Sutters moved to Washington D.C. and Sutter spent the next several years petitioning Congress for restitution for the property he felt had been taken from him in California. He received a small pension as reimbursement of taxes he had paid after the annexation. The couple lived at Lititz Springs, Pennsylvania, where he died in 1880.

In California, Sutter's Fort fell to decay, neglected as the new city of Sacramento grew up nearby. The main building, which had been Sutter's home and office, and had been variously used as a storehouse, boarding house, retail store and even a chicken hatchery, is the only original part of the fort remaining. The massive walls were left to crumble, the adobe bricks taken away for building sites or road construction. In 1862 what remained of the walls was washed away by heavy flooding. In 1891, the site was purchased by the historical organization Native Sons of the Golden West for $20,000. The fort was reconstructed on a slightly smaller footprint and donated to the State of California as part of the State Park System in 1947. Today, the State Historic Park operates as a living history museum and is a regular field trip destination for California schoolchildren.

In the end, the "Emperor of California" had watched his empire evaporate, over-shadowed by every enterprise Samuel Brannan undertook. Brannan's overarching ambition and keen business sense trumped Sutter's focus on land acquisition and dependence upon Native American labor as means to wealth. Prior to the discovery at Sutter's Mill, Sutter's dream had endured and grown. With the advent of the Gold Rush, however, all Sutter's plans were set asunder by the Forty Niners while everything Brannan touched seemed to turn to gold. Once good friends, the two men became bitter rivals. Sutter became increasingly jealous, even challenging Brannan's foundational Mormon beliefs. As Brannan's Sacramento blossomed, Sutter's rival town project of Sutterville floundered. The final indignity was Brannan's domination of Sutter's son August and ultimate transfer of much of the former Sutter properties to the Brannan portfolio, paying only a fraction of the negotiated price.

Ever supportive in print of the ventures of his former boss, **Edward Kemble** continued to build the readership base of the *Alta California*. Active in San Francisco civic affairs, Kemble also followed Brannan to Sacramento and established the *Placer Times* during the early days of the Gold Rush, bringing with him the original old press that had been used in Monterey. Kemble later recalled this first publishing venture north of San Francisco:

> *"It was late in the evening when the party, without any further adventure than a thorough sousing overboard from a canoe, in attempting to cross the 'lake' at Sutterville, arrived at the Fort. But late as it was, the arrival of the press was celebrated that night with oysters and champagne, in one of the old rooms within the adobe walls....On the 28th of April 1849, appeared the first number of the pioneer journal of Sacramento, and the interior of the State."*[3]

Before leaving for a trip east in October 1849, Kemble was feted at a gala dinner, attended by representatives of the fledgling journalism community in the West, where he was celebrated as "The Father of the California Press." Kemble was yet only 22 years old. The *Alta California* office and equipment were destroyed in 1851 by one of early San Francisco's many fires. Following the death of his business partner, Edward Gilbert, also one of California's first congressmen, who was killed in a duel with James Denver over political editorials, Kemble left for extended travel in Europe, where he served as the *Alta's* first foreign correspondent. In New York, Kemble served on the Committee for Pacific Coast Emigration, before returning to California, writing and editing for *The California Chronicle* and *Sacramento Union*. In 1858, he anonymously published his landmark *A History of California Newspapers, 1846 – 1858,* based on questionnaires distributed to all periodicals in the state. The *Alta* called it

> *"The longest article we have ever seen in any paper, and a valuable contribution to the literature and history of the state."*[4]

The following day, *the San Francisco Times* wrote:

> *"As a whole, the work is an admirable performance and evinces great industry and careful research on the part of the writer."*[5]

Although the study was widely referenced by scholars and journalists, it appeared without Kemble's authorship being recognized until 1927.

In 1855, Kemble married Cecelia Amanda Windsor. The couple had two children, including Edward Windsor Kemble, later a cartoonist with the *New York Herald, New York Sun* and *Harper's Weekly*. During the Civil War, Kemble served as

Paymaster for the Union Army in the Department of Virginia, breveted out as a lieutenant colonel at war's end. He later served as Inspector for Indian Affairs under President U.S. Grant and spent four years running the west coast bureau in the Associated Press office in New York. He continued as correspondent to the *San Francisco Call, San Francisco Bulletin* and *Sacramento Record Union*. Edward Kemble died at Mott Haven, New York in 1886 at age 57. At the time of publication in 1858, Kemble's *History* listed for San Francisco 12 daily newspapers, 17 weeklies, four monthlies and four semi-monthlies, as well as reprinted editions of several papers produced for distribution elsewhere in California and distributed by steamer to the Atlantic States and Europe.[4.] California journalism had evolved quickly since Edward Kemble, as a teenage non-Mormon apprentice printer, had followed Sam Brannan on an epic sea journey and hauled a printing press ashore at Yerba Buena. His reluctance to jump on the gold discovery story notwithstanding, Kemble played a large part in building San Francisco.

As **Sam Brannan's** business interests multiplied and expanded, his personal life became increasingly chaotic. He was joined in California by his brother, John, and the pair embarked on several business ventures, until John Brannan's untimely death while sailing to China in 1862. Brannan's sister, Mary Ann Badlam, and her family also migrated to California. Although Brannan had differences with her husband Alexander Badlam, he nevertheless remained close to his nephew Alexander Badlam Jr., who became prominent in insurance, railroading and politics, and became Brannan's executor at the end of his life. Brannan continued to vocally condemn the Mormon practice of polygamy but he, himself, was a serial womanizer. His affairs ranged from anonymous assignations to enduring emotional romances. He lavished favors upon the actress Lola Montez as he publicly squired her around town. In 1855, Brannan covertly returned from New York with his first wife Harriet Hatch and their grown daughter Almira, and secretly supported them in California until Hattie obtained a legal divorce. At home, Ann Eliza Brannan suffered the humiliation of her husband's philandering and his increasingly frequent drinking bouts.

Unlike her devout mother, Brannan's wife had never accepted her husband's religious practices and was relieved when he ended his association with the Church. Brannan's great wealth provided his family with affluence and social status. However, she was unable to acclimate to life in San Francisco, despite the elegant house, furnishings, carriage, wealth and other amenities Brannan provided her. In an effort to appease his wife, Brannan took his family on an extended grand tour of Europe, following which his wife and children remained in Paris, where the children were schooled. Brannan hoped the stay in the glittering capitals and culture of Europe would appease his unhappy wife and reduce the tension in their marriage. It did not. Upon her return, Mrs. Brannan sued for divorce in 1868, insisting upon a half-million-dollar cash settlement as her half of the estate. Since most of Brannan's fortune was tied up in land, he was forced to sell property at great loss during a severe economic downturn. Mrs. Brannan apparently mismanaged her windfall by investing poorly in Comstock Lode mining stock. Always ambitious for wealth, Ann Eliza Corwin Brannan saw a vast fortune come and go.

She died impoverished in San Francisco in 1898. Brannan's losses brought on more drinking and precipitated the downward spiral of his financial fortunes. He would blame his former wife for the estrangement of his children.

Not all of Brannan's ventures turned golden. His Midas Touch failed when he backed an abortive 1852 coup in the Sandwich Islands which would have installed himself as governor general. The plot fizzled with almost comic opera overtones as the various players refused to perform their roles as directed. The plotters were further disgraced by the revelation they had illegally plundered sacks of U.S. mail on the steamship between Hawai'i and the mainland. The misadventure more closely resembled a drunken casino cruise than a paramilitary expedition and Brannan was met with jeers of derision upon return to San Francisco.

A gregarious joiner, Brannan helped found and finance the Society of California Pioneers, but his efforts to join the Masonic Order were stymied. Intrigued by similarities between Mormon ritual and aspects of the Masonic rite, Brannan pledged several lodges, only to be blackballed for his character and lifestyle. His brawling was as well-known as his drinking, the pair not unrelated, but when sober, he was everyone's friend. He ultimately joined a Masonic lodge out-of-state, as well as founded an Odd Fellows Lodge. His places of business were also halls of political maneuvering, social gaiety and lunchtime watering holes for the affluent and the aspiring of The City.

Brannan's focus became increasingly scattered, and he paid less and less attention to detail, often delegating management to his brother John or nephew Alexander Badlam

Jr. Much of his time was spent defending the multitude of lawsuits that came at him; several attorneys enjoyed comfortable retirements after their association with Sam Brannan. He flirted with politics, being elected state senator, but resigning almost immediately. In the midst of the financial panic of 1857, he started a bank on cheap money borrowed in New York and lent in San Francisco at high interest. He followed with the Pacific Accumulation Loan Company despite the venture being hugely undercapitalized and made it successful. On the eve of the Civil War, Brannan renounced his long relationship with the Democratic Party over abolition and became a fervent supporter of Abraham Lincoln, being a Lincoln delegate in 1864 representing the California Union Party, a coalition of political interests. He sponsored a volunteer fire brigade and purchased a silver-plated fire engine valued at some $10,000. He was an early investor in the transcontinental railroad; his stake in the Central Pacific Railroad was once greater than any of the so-called "Big Four" of Stanford, Hopkins, Huntington and Crocker. Brannan also built California's second railroad, the Sacramento – Folsom line, and later a spur between Napa and Calistoga.

Development of Calistoga – formed from the names California and Saratoga – consumed Brannan's attention and fortune. It also nearly cost him his life. The special edition of *The California Star*, as early as 1847, had trumpeted the wonders of the Napa Valley. Brannan sought to develop a world-class resort around the hot springs found there (which reminded him of Saratoga, New York.) He poured millions of dollars into the project, building a hotel, surrounded by pools, gardens, a horse farm, brandy distillery and residential lots for sale. Brannan also introduced European varietal grapes to the Napa Valley creating the first vineyard there. One evening, attempting to evict squatters on his Calistoga property, Brannan sustained eight gunshot wounds in an explosive shootout. With Irish luck and the best available medical care, Brannan recovered, although his crippled body and health would be compromised from then on. In the end, the Calistoga project proved too small to attract enough clientele or investors. Lenders foreclosed and subsequent efforts to revive the project failed, forcing Brannan to sell at bargain prices. Leland Stanford, it is said, considered the site for his proposed university. Author Robert Louis Stevenson penned *The Silverado Squatters* while honeymooning there. Brannan's dream was left in ruin. Today visitors still enjoy the Calistoga hot springs, and the Napa Valley is one of the premier wine regions of the world.

Brannan became increasingly despondent over his health and financial misfortune. By 1870, most of his agricultural and business real estate had been sold or repossessed. Much of his fortune had been consumed by his divorce settlement, debt service and bad deals. In 1865, Brannan had supported the efforts of Benito Juárez in his resistance to the French invasion of Mexico and the rule of the Hapsburg Maximilian. He underwrote several million dollars of Mexican bonds at a cost of $30,000. In a weak bond market, Brannan agreed to take over all the bonds with his initial investment returned. The Mexican government rejected his terms, offering hundreds of thousands of acres of Sonora desert land instead. Brannan would spend most of his remaining years as a land speculator trying to entice investors and immigrants to settle in Sonora.

He established the Sonoran Colonization Association of New York, headed by his old friend and former editor Edward C. Kemble. He even sought to attract groups of Latter-Day Saints looking for a refuge where they could practice polygamy, however the Church had no intention of doing business with the notorious Sam Brannan. Brannan's attempts to legalize his Mexican land grants collapsed and the fierce resistance by the hostile, indigenous Yaqui Indians, who hated colonization attempts by both Mexicans and Anglo-Americans, proved too great an obstacle. His adventures in Mexico, while supportive of republicanism, also fell into the pattern of 19th century American filibustering in Latin America, plotting to carve out territory by any means necessary that could ultimately be annexed by the United States. Brannan settled in the port city of Guaymas on the Sea of Cortés (Gulf of California) and married a wealthy younger woman named Carmelita Carmen de Llaguno in 1882. His health returned somewhat, and he seldom drank liquor.

Ever the promoter, Brannan remained convinced arid Sonora would become the spring from which wealth would flow. By the mid-1880s he still envisioned establishing an independent Sonoran Empire, much as he had once dreamt of doing in California and Hawai'i. He rekindled a relationship with his son, Samuel Jr., who had been educated in mining engineering in Europe and who became entangled in his father's schemes. He continued to rail against The Church and polygamy, never mentioning his own early plural marriage. He retained his eternal optimism for his own ventures as well as for the world, as evidenced in his letter to life-long friend Jesse Little:

"Truth will triumph over bigotry and fantanticism [sic] and facts will take its place and mankind will be forced by reason to become enlightened."[7]

But the efforts to substantiate his Mexican land claims had worn him down. Living alone – Carmen had refused to follow him and play nursemaid – he sold pencils door-to-door in Nogales in 1887 before settling on a small farm at Escondido, in northern San Diego County. He spent his last days as an old farmer tending his citrus grove before a bowel ailment ended his life on May 5, 1889. Brannan's corpse remained unclaimed in a San Diego vault for more than a year until Alexander Badlam Jr. arranged for its burial at Mount Hope Cemetery in San Diego. His grave remained unmarked until 1926, his then-donated headstone reading:

SAM BRANNAN
1819–1889
CALIFORNIA PIONEER OF '46
DREAMER – LEADER
AND
EMPIRE-BUILDER

The press of the day duly recognized Brannan's passing. In a lengthy obituary under the headline *"The Pioneer At Rest,"* The *San Francisco Examiner* called him *"One of the Strangest and Most Remarkable of Men."*[8]

The *Examiner* recalled Brannan's days as publisher at the dawn of the Gold Rush:

"In May 1848, Brannan, in a measure, came to grief with the Star. Not from any loss of business popularity, but from the simple circumstance that

everybody in the office except himself – printers, foremen, devil and all, dropped rule and composing stick and rushed away to the mines. Calmly Brannan took the bull by the horns, suspended publication – he could, indeed, do nothing else – and quietly slipped away to the mines to see for himself what was in the glittering tales. What conclusion he came to was evident."[9]

Contemporary historian John S. Hitell published a lengthy piece in the *Overland Monthly Magazine*. He concluded:

"[When he died...] he was no longer a leader in public subscriptions, in popular excitements, in building railroads, or in erecting costly homes, But his memory will long remain as that of a man of strong character and much influence in the early development of our State, a man whose career and its close deserve mention in a magazine which strives to make the history of California familiar to its people, and especially to its younger generation and newcomers who have no direct knowledge of the events that occurred in the first ten years after the American conquest. During that period, Mr. Brannan was one of the leading Californians, in some respects second to none. Peace to his ashes."[10]

The Church publication, *Deseret Evening News*, announced *"Sam Brannan Gone."* The reporter wrote:

"He was once a "Mormon" [quotation marks theirs] *and obtained some prominence in early times, as he took a company by water from New York to San Francisco and wanted our people to settle on the coast. His course and habits were not consistent with the life of a Latter-Day Saint, and so he was disconnected with the Church and plunged into the speculations and excitements of pioneer California experience...He had some redeeming qualities, and it is to be hoped that these will outweigh the faults that were manifested in his adventurous and eventful life. Poor Sam! Will be the general expression over the news of his departure to another sphere."*[11]

With his death evolved more of the Brannan legend. One popular story claimed he had at long last received some $40,000 in back interest and principal from the Mexican government, with which he settled his remaining debts and thus died debt-free. There is no record of this happening. A second story, also apocryphal and not surprisingly also involving money, has a dying Brannan borrowing a 20-dollar gold piece to spite Apostle Parley Pratt, who had prophesied Brannan would die penniless.

History has not been overly kind to Samuel Brannan. In many ways this dominant figure has been marginalized and reduced to almost cartoonish caricature: dancing jig-like in the middle of Portsmouth Square with his bottle of gold dust in one hand and waving his beaver hat in the other. The eminent 19th century historian H.H. Bancroft, from whom almost all California history flowed, paid scant attention to Brannan and even less to the considerable aggregate accomplishments of early California Mormons. Most subsequent scholarship on Brannan has been done by church researchers, historians and writers with access to whatever primary historical record exists, but often with their own point of view. Even within that particular religious community, where Sam Brannan should rank only behind Joseph Smith and Brigham Young in 19th century historical significance, Brannan has, of course, been dropped from the pantheon of Saints to almost footnote status, except by a handful of objective church scholars. And San Francisco, the city that owes its origin to Brannan, has done a woeful job of memorializing him, with only a street name and few plaques, but little else.

Elsewhere, Brannan is remembered in Sacramento, where his rebuilt home can be visited in the Old Town and a middle school bears his name. Historical markers can be found in other towns he also founded: Yuba City and Calistoga. Calistoga also offers a Brannan Inn, Brannan Center and Brannan store site. Scattered throughout the Mother Lode are Brannan Island, Brannan Bluff, Brannan Creek, Brannan Mountain, Brannan Spring and Brannan River. In 1872, his son Samuel Jr., a natural history enthusiast, collected a marine snail species at Santa Barbara Island and named it *Siphonaria brannani Stearn* after his father. These gastropods are classified as simultaneously hermaphrodites; randy Sam Brannan would no doubt have found that amusing.

In 1887, Sam Brannan had made a brief return visit to San Francisco. Crippled and ill, he walked the hills with difficulty using a cane. He stopped at buildings he had once owned and grand hotels he could no longer afford to stay at.

Grizzled and grey, his face punished by partial paralysis from a stroke, few recognized the aged pioneer who once had straddled San Francisco like a colossus. The cold damp fog enveloped his gaunt frame and tormented his aching joints. He quickly departed The City, retreating to warmer climes. A century later, the quintessential San Francisco rock band, the Jefferson Airplane, rebranded as Starship, joyously sang of building the city on rock-n-roll. Of course, it had actually been built on gold. Built by the thousands who answered the siren song heralded by Samuel Brannan in his little newspaper, *The California Star.* Brannan was The City's first architect, its master mason, its biggest, most outrageous promoter. He had started it all on the sandy cove of the Great Bay at Yerba Buena.

Notes

1. "Arrest of a Robber!" *Alta California,* June 11, 1851.

2. Eugene C. Campbell, "The Apostasy of Samuel Brannan," *Utah Historical Quarterly,* vol. 27, no. 2, 1959, https://issuu.com>uhq_volume27_1959_number2, retrieved March 29, 2023.

3. Edward C. Kemble and Helen Harding Bretnor (ed.), <u>A History of Newspapers in California 1846 – 1858</u>, Los Gatos, CA: Talisman Press, 1962, p. 137.

4. *Alta California*, December 27, 1858.

5. *San Francisco Times,* December 28, 1858.

6. *Kemble, op. cit.*, p. 132.

7. Samuel Brannan, Letter to Jesse Little, June 6, 1887, Brannan papers, BYU Archives.

8. *San Francisco Examiner*, May 7, 1889, pp. 3-4.

9. <u>Ibid</u>.

10. John S. Hittell, "Samuel Brannan," *Overland Monthly*, June 1889, pp. 648-50.

11. "Sam Brannan Gone," *Deseret Evening News,* May 9, 1889.

Afterword
Searching for Yerba Buena

I t is still dark as I step onto the sidewalk on Market Street. It will be another hour before daylight crawls hesitatingly over the Berkeley Hills and skips across the bay into San Francisco. Even then, the sun may not cut the gloom until much later in the morning. Cradling a warm coffee cup in both hands, I wait for the caffeine to kick in. In both directions, brightly colored bundles lie motionless along the broad boulevard, the sleeping bags and tents of San Francisco's unhoused citizens of the street. In the street, blocking the entrance to a valet parking lane, a pair of legs protrude from a cardboard shelter, a curled human figure underneath seeking warmth escaping up from a manhole cover in the asphalt. The homeless crisis, so decried by so many of San Francisco's critics, thankfully seems to retreat as we walk farther away from its concentration along the Market Street corridor and Tenderloin neighborhood. But it is a sadness with no apparent solution.

Today's expedition will search for evidence of a pre-Gold Rush Yerba Buena. My companion and guide is Tom Graham, long-time reporter for the *San Francisco Chronicle* and journalism instructor at City College of San Francisco. Tom is best known for having walked every block of every street in The City. He serialized his seven-year, 2,000-mile, 2,612 street odyssey for his readers in the *Chron*. Sharing my

191

interest in California history, as well as a mutual curiosity about early San Francisco journalism, Tom and I head out. Reminders abound that The City was originally founded as a pious homage to that Catholic saint of Assisi: The St. Francis Hotel sits majestically guarding Union Square; a good friend was a long-time member of St. Francis Yacht Club; and, of course, down Bush Street is St. Francis Hospital where I made my own debut too many years ago. The saint's name in Spanish, *San Francisco,* is ubiquitous. What will we find of that other Saint, the Latter-Day one who traded his religion for everything else California had to offer?

By coincidence, today is the anniversary of the great 1906 earthquake and fire. A small knot of early risers has gathered in the pre-dawn at Lotta's Fountain at the triangle formed by Market, Kearny and Geary Streets to memorialize the event. The cast iron column, which served as a gathering point for many displaced by the earthquake and which many now consider an eye-sore, was donated by actress Lotta Crabtree, a one-time protege of Lola Montez, Brannan's sometime mistress – so there's a connection. The fire bell rings at 5:12 a.m. A large floral wreath of roses is laid by the monument. But it seems a tradition that is slipping away. There no longer are any survivors who remember that day when the earth shook, and the sky burned.

Exploring old Yerba Buena today requires an active imagination and a good historical guidebook. We consult Daniel Bacon's informative and entertaining *Walking San Francisco on the Barbary Coast Trail.* Almost nothing remains of pre-Gold Rush days. Some buildings still show the red brick facades that replaced the earlier wooden structures which so often burned down, but even those brick walls came after the Gold Rush. And, of course, this entire northeast corner of The City was largely destroyed in the fire of 1906 that followed the quake. The neighborhood which now encompasses The City's financial district sets in the shadows of looming high-rise office towers including the iconic Transamerica Pyramid, once The City's tallest building. Sunlight struggles to slither through the concrete and glass canyons. The streets take on the names of Mexican War–era military leaders: Montgomery, Kearny, Stockton. Grant's name would replace Dupont's following the Civil War.

Between Montgomery and Sansome Streets, at the end of an alley bearing his name, we find a plaque to William Leidesdorff, another early Yerba Buena entrepreneur and civic leader who died at the start of the Gold Rush. We walk along Montgomery Street, the original shoreline of the bay. Today it is some seven blocks up from the bay, land reclaimed by years of infill. In one alley, a wavy design in the pavement marks the original waterline. It seems eerie to know we are walking over the graveyard of scores of Gold Rush-era ships, abandoned and left to rot in the mudflats and serve as landfill and foundations of future buildings. Excavators still discover shards of ships' hulls and cargoes buried beneath the financial district. We push on to cross the Kearny Street pedestrian overpass leading to the epicenter of San Francisco history: the old Yerba Buena Plaza, now Portsmouth Square.

Located in the heart of Chinatown, Portsmouth Square buzzes with community energy. Although the neighborhood's children are in school, the square is filled with adult Chinese residents practicing *tai chi* and otherwise enjoying the mild morning. We find the site of the old Mexican adobe Customs House from 1846. A monument at the southwest corner locates the site of the first public school in California, built in 1848. On the opposite corner of the square another plaque describes the rising of the American flag there by marines from the USS *Portsmouth* in 1846. A flagpole rises from that spot, but today no flag waves from the pole. Surrounding the plaza are the sites of the Old Custom House, the Portsmouth Hotel and the locations where Sam Brannan yelled *"Gold!, Gold!"* and later called for vigilante justice.

Leaving the square, on Washington Street we come across a brightly painted pagoda-style building wedged between a Chinese restaurant and a souvenir shop. The building houses the East-West Bank, but a careful search finds the plaque embedded in the bank's front step. We have come to the original site of Brannan's home and office of *The California Star*. It seems an understated tribute to this nativity of California history and journalism birth.

The plaque, obscured by time and wear reads:

ON THIS SITE JANUARY 9, 1847
THE CALIFORNIA STAR THE FIRST
NEWSPAPER IN SAN FRANCISCO
WAS PUBLISHED BY SAMULEL BRANNAN
THIS MARKER PLACED BY E CLAMPUS VITUS
FEBRUARY 6, 1939

We march up to Grant Avenue, farther into Chinatown. Merchants have rolled up the iron grates in front of their shops. We see the succulent ducks hanging in fogged restaurant windows. Grocery patrons are busy with daily shopping and the *dim sum* restaurants are already crowded. Stores of fine Asian art seem to merge with the tacky souvenir stands and emporiums of Chinese herbal medicines. Bright red Chinese lanterns are strung across the alleys and laundry hangs from iron balconies and fire escapes. I notice several Taiwanese national flags flying from rooftops. It all seems, at the same time, both grotesquely touristy and incredibly authentic. When the original residents headed for the gold fields, the Chinese occupied their deserted homes as squatters and remained. I wonder what Sam Brannan would have made of Chinatown. He was selectively racist. On the one hand he was a life-long abolitionist and even formed a Black militia troop. He befriended the *Californios*, married a Mexican woman and spent most of his later life in Mexico. But Brannan was virulently anti-Chinese. He advocated for harsh exclusionary laws and restrictive policies. How would he have received this community of *Celestials* who came for the Gold Mountain, built the railroad, suffered serious discrimination yet thrived to become an integral part of The City's social and civic fabric?

On Grant Avenue, near Clay Street at number 823, we find a modest bronze wall plaque almost hidden at the narrow entrance to an apartment building. It reads **"The birthplace of a great city."** Here, or within a few yards of this plaque, the Northern Federation of Civic Organizations of San Francisco recognized the site of William Richardson's Casa Grande, the first adobe dwelling at Yerba Buena Cove in 1835-1836. It is an underwhelming memorial.

Veering off from Chinatown, we stop at a Vietnamese noodle house, as authentic as any in Saigon or Hanoi. The Vietnamese, of course, are relatively new immigrants to The

City, arriving in the late 1970s as political refugees following the collapse of their U.S.-backed South Vietnam to the communists. Over pungent *pho,* I recall volunteering at the Presidio when the first airlifted Vietnamese orphan babies arrived in 1975. Many of those orphans, now in middle-age, own their own piece of San Francisco themselves and are sending their own children to Berkeley and Stanford, as the Vietnamese community thrives in this Pacific Rim melting pot.

On Broadway we turn toward the bay. Between Battery and Front Streets, we discover the plaque commemorating where it all began with the landing of the *Brooklyn* in 1846. Unlike Plymouth Rock on the east coast, which is now covered by rising sea water at high tide (Plymouth Rock has been relocated several times over the centuries, but Plymouth Harbor has risen a foot and a half since measurement began), this point in Yerba Buena was once the farthest rocky tip of the cove into the bay but is now three blocks inland. We wonder if rising sea levels will someday once again reclaim parts of Yerba Buena.

Erected in 1940 by The Daughters of Utah Pioneers, the plaque reads:

SHIP BROOKLYN

COMMEMORATING THE LANDING AT THIS POINT OF THE SHIP BROOKLYN JULY 31, 1846. A 370 TON VESSEL CARRYING MORMON COLONISTS AND CREW OF NEARLY 300 UNDER THE LEADERSHIP OF SAMUEL BRANNAN

IN THE HOLD WAS A PRINTING PRESS, 179 BOOKS FOR EDUCATIONAL PURPOSES, TWO COMPLETE FLOUR MILLS, PLOWS, HARROWS AND A SUPPLY OF IMPLEMENTS FOR SETTLING THE NEW COUNTRY.

There is also a plaque memorializing the arrival of the *Brooklyn* on the grounds of the Latter-Day Saints Temple grounds across the bay in the Oakland Hills.

We climb the cardio-challenging Filbert Steps up the steep east face of Telegraph Hill to Coit Tower to take in the panoramic view of what was once Yerba Buena. After months of reading and writing, and then walking the streets of Yerba Buena, it still seems difficult to reconstruct the empty cove set among the sand dunes, the derelict Presidio and the isolated Spanish mission first encountered by Brannan and his pilgrims in 1846. It's equally hard to wrap my head around how San Francisco became an instant city with the discovery of gold two years later. But I know it happened, I can read about it in *The California Star.*

In today's usage Yerba Buena would not refer to the pre-Gold Rush hamlet, but rather the island in San Francisco Bay supporting the San Francisco-Oakland Bay Bridge. The island, known during Gold Rush days as Goat Island, was renamed Yerba Buena in the 1930s, before it hosted the Golden Gate Exposition of 1939. The island's extension, known as Treasure Island, was a major U.S. Naval facility from which a couple million service personnel shipped out during World War II. Treasure Island was decommissioned in 1997 and leased to San

Francisco for commercial use. Plans for Yerba Buena Island call for private development of homes, hotels, a ferry terminal, along with parkland and major investment in public art. Yerba Buena today also could refer to Yerba Buena Gardens, a popular South of Market arts, cultural and recreation center.

Along the Embarcadero at 101 Spear Street in the former Rincon Annex U.S. Post Office, now a commercial center, a series of San Francisco historical paintings are on display. Created in the 1940s by artist Anton Refregier as part of a federal WPA project, the panels became controversial during the era of McCarthyism and anti-communist fever. Panel number 9, *"An Early Newspaper Office"* depicts an unidentified figure, presumably Samuel Brannan, reading a copy of *The California Star.*

As for the great bay, itself, today almost all shipping to northern California is handled by the larger Port of Oakland rather than San Francisco. Dredging continues around the clock to remove mud and silt from the shallow bay floor to accommodate ever-larger container ships and to help restore shoreline wetlands as a first line of defense against rising sea levels. Environmentally, the bay is healthier now than in several decades, despite pressures from industrial, developmental and recreational interests.

The Bay Area's newly formed professional National Women's Soccer League team has chosen to call itself simply Bay FC (Football Club), a fitting nod to the timeless influence of the bay on the entire region.

There does, however, remain one more area linking us to Sam Brannan. "South of the slot" (the slot being the trench for the buried cable that once pulled the cable cars along Market Street) – where the Embarcadero wraps around the bay shore, is the foot of Brannan Street. At 1 Brannan Street, half a dozen bronze historical markers are embedded in the tree-shaded sidewalk. The first establishes Brannan's name on the new street by the U.S. Topographical Engineers in 1853. Other plaques reproduce his likeness and highlight some biography. These are followed by the original Seal of the San Francisco Committee of Vigilance and a quotation:

> *"Some contend that there are really no laws in force here, but the divine law, and the law of nature."*

> – Sam Brannan, Editor California Star. March 27, 1847

In talking about San Francisco, he had described himself.

FIN

William Briggs

Acknowledgements

Among the many who encouraged and enabled this book, two people deserve my deepest appreciation. From the start, my cousin Christy and her husband Alan Johansen grasped the significance of this less well-known nugget of California history and my desire to objectively retell it. She immediately began sourcing reference material for me from her personal library and from within the LDS community. Together they vetted my manuscript for accuracy of their church history. I deeply value their contribution and our family connection.

Secondly, a huge shout out to good friend Tom Graham whose passion for San Francisco recalls renowned *San Francisco Chronicle* columnist Herb Caen. (Indeed, Tom once edited Caen's columns). A great journalist and journalism educator in his own right, with the stamina of a Sherpa and the pen of a poet, Tom likely knows San Francisco as well as anyone from walking every street. As my guide in both San Francisco and Old Sacramento, Tom proved an incredible host, repository of vast knowledge and true friend. For all that as well as his graciously provided foreword, I am in his debt.

Some of this material was previously presented at the 2023 Latter-Day Saints and Media Studies Symposium for which I had the pleasure of collaborating with a former SJSU colleague and friend Dr. Ken Plowman, now at Brigham Young University. It was a joy working with him again.

William Briggs

Special appreciation goes to the various docents and librarians who facilitated access to all the research., including at Cal-Press Foundation; San Mateo County Historical Foundation; California Society of Pioneers; California Historical Society; Bancroft Library U.C. Berkeley; Sacramento History Museum; Sutter's Fort State Historic Park; and California Digital Newspaper Collection and California Museum of Photography, both at U.C. Riverside.

Writing a trilogy of California histories has enabled me to continue working with talented designer Briana Carlson Monaco, whose eye for color and style is superb. And once again, thank you to Emily Veeh and the folks at Bookstand Publishing for their patience and professionalism. Brad Jones and Cinda Meister at Booksmart, Morgan Hill, continue to be great support and friends. Thank you all.

As always, I am buoyed by my supportive family. I love you all. Let these stories remind our grandchildren of their heritage, and occasionally remind them of me.

Selected Bibliography

Books

Arax, Mark, The Dreamt Land. Chasing Water and Dust Across California, New York: Vintage Books, 2019.

Bacon, Daniel, Walking San Francisco on the Barbary Coast Trail, San Francisco: Quicksilver Press, 2013.

Bagley, Will, Scoundrel's Tale, The Samuel Brannan Papers, Logan UT: Utah State University Press, 1999.

Bancroft, H.H., History of California, 7 vols. San Francisco: The History Co., 1886-1890.

Brands, H.W., The Age of Gold. The California Gold Rush and the New American Dream, New York: Anchor Books, 2002.

Browning, Peter, ed., San Francisco. Yerba Buena. From Beginning to the Gold Rush 1769 – 1849, Lafayette CA: Great Western Books, 1998.

Cole, Tom, A Short History of San Francisco, Berkeley: Heyday, 2015 (Kindle ed.).

Cowan, Richard O., and Homer, William E., California Saints: A 150-Year Legacy in the Golden State, Provo UT: Religious Studies Center, Brigham Young University, 1996.

Crowley, David and Heyer, Paul, Communication in History, 6th ed., Boston: Allyn & Bacon, 2011.

Dana, Richard Henry, Jr., Two Years Before the Mast, originally published New York: Harper and Bros., 1840. Kindle electronic edition 2022.

Dickson, Samuel, <u>Tales of San Francisco,</u> Stanford, CA: Stanford University Press, 1960.

Emery, Michael, Emery, Edwin, and Roberts, Nancy L., <u>The Press in America. An Interpretive History of the Mass Media,</u> 9th ed., Boston: Allyn & Bacon, 2000.

Faragher, John Mark, <u>California. An American History,</u> New Haven CT: Yale University Press, 2022.

Hayes, Derek, <u>Historical Atlas of California,</u> Oakland: University of California Press, 2007.

Farris, Glen J., (ed.) <u>So Far From Home. Russians in Early California,</u> Berkeley CA: Heyday, 2012.

Fellow, Anthony R., <u>American Media History,</u> 3rd ed.., Boston: Wadsworth, 2013.

Folkerts, Jean and Teeter, Dwight L., Jr., <u>Voices of a Nation. A History of Mass Media in the United States,</u> 4th ed., Boston: Allyn & Bacon, 2002.

Fracchia, Charles A., <u>When the waters came up to Montgomery Street: San Francisco During the Gold Rush,</u> Virginia Beach, VA: Donning Co., 2009.

Kamiya, Gary, <u>Cool Gray City of Love. 49 Views of San Francisco,</u> New York: Bloomsbury, 2013.

_____, (introduction), <u>The End of the Golden Gate. Writers on Loving and (Sometimes) Leaving San Francisco.</u> San Francisco: Chronicle Prism, 2021.

Kemble, Edward Cleveland and Bretnor, Helen Harding, ed., <u>A History of California Newspapers, 1846 – 1858,</u> Los Gatos CA: The Talisman Press, 1962.

Matthews, Owen, <u>Glorious Misadventures. Nikolai Rezanov and the Dream of a Russian America,</u> New York: Bloomsbury, 2013.

Meldahl, Keith Heyer, Hard Road West. History and Geology along the Gold Rush Trail, Chicago: University of Chicago Press, 2008.

Merry, Robert W., A Country of Vast Designs. James K. Polk, the Mexican War and the Conquest of the American Continent, New York: Simon &. Shuster, 2009.

Owens, Kenneth N., Gold Rush Saints. California Mormons and the Great Rush for Riches, Norman OK: University of Oklahoma Press, 2004.

Richards, Leonard L., The California Gold Rush and the Coming of the Civil War, New York: Alfred A. Knopf, 2007.

Ricketts, Norma Baldwin, The California Star 1847-1848. San Francisco's First Newspaper, Mesa AZ: Postal Instant Press, 1996.

Rogers, Fred Blackburn (introduction), The California Star. Yerba Buena and San Francisco, vol. 1, 1847-1848, Berkeley: Howell North Books, 1965.

Sherman, William Tecumseh, Memoirs of General William Tecumseh Sherman by Himself, New York: Penguin Classics, 2000.

Starr, Kevin, California. A History, New York: The Modern Library, 2007.

Stellman, Louis J., Sam Brannan. Builder of San Francisco, New York: Exposition Press, 1953.

Stevenson Robert L., Global Communication in the Twenty-First Century, New York: Longman, 1994.

Sweat, Anthony, Mormons. An Open Book, Salt Lake City UT: Ensign Peak, 2012.

Vancouver, George, A Voyage of Discovery to the North Pacific Ocean and Round the World In Which the Coast of

North-West America has been carefully Examined and Accurately Surveyed, Undertaken by HIS MAJESTY'S Command, principally with a view to ascertain the existence of any navigable communication between the North Pacific and North Atlantic Oceans and performed in the years 1790, 1791, 1792, 1793 1794 and 1795 in the Discovery sloop of war and armed tender Chatham under the Command of Captain George Vancouver, originally published in London for G.G. and J. Robinson and j. Edwards, 1798; W. Lamb (ed.), Milton Park, England: Routledge, 1984.

Wilcox, Dennis L., and Cameron, Glen T., Public Relations Strategies and Tactics, 9th ed., Boston: Pearson, 2009.

Winchester, Simon, Land. How the Hunger for Ownership Shaped the Modern World, New York: Harper Perennial, 2021.

Articles and Digital Sources

Albertson, Dean, "The Discovery of Gold in California as Viewed by New York and London", *The Pacific Spectato*r, vol. III, Number I, The Museum of the City of San Francisco, Winter 1949.

Anonymous, "The Apostasy of Samuel Brannan," https://lisuu.com>uhq_vol 27_1959_number2.

_____ "History of the Presidio," Presidio Trust, https://www.presidio.gov.

_____ "Mormon Battalion," California Pioneer Heritage Foundation, https://californiapioneers.com>historic-events>mormon-battalion.

_____. "The Persecution of the Mormons," Constitutional Rights Foundation, Bill of Right in Action (17:1), Winter 2000, https://www.crf-usa.org/.

_____,"Samuel Brannan: Gold Rush Entrepreneur," *American Experience,* https://www.pbs.org/wgbh/americanexperience/features/goldrush-samuel-brannan.

_____ "Samuel Brannan and the Eastern Saints," BYU Religious Studies Center, https://rsc.byu.edu/california-saints/samuel-brannan-eastern-saints.

_____ "Samuel Brannan: The Mormon Leader in California Matched Wits with Brigham Young," *LDSLiving,* July 15, 2013. https://www.ldsliving.com/samuel-brannan-the-mormon-leader-matched-wits-with-brigham-young/s/73095.

Beyl, Ernest, "The Evolution of San Francisco Newspapers from 1846, Part 2, *Marina Times,* Sept. 2013, https://www.marinatimes.com>theevolutionofsanfrancisconewspapers from 1846.

"The Brannan Family," The Saunders Family History, Chapter 9, revised Jan. 2021, http://www.saundersfamilyhistory.com>images.

Breschini, Gary S., "The First Newspaper in California," Monterey Historical Society, 2000, http://mchmuseum.com>firstpaper.

Elder, William "Where the Plates Meet," European Geoscience Union, EGU Blogs, Nov. 30, 2020, https://blogs.egu.eu>divisions>2020/11/30.

Everett, Amelia D., "The Ship Brooklyn," *California Historical Quarterly*, vol. 37, no. 3, Sept. 1958, pp. 229-240.

Graham, Tom, "Tom Graham walks every street in San Francisco," *sfgate,* July 11, 2010, https://www.sfgate.com/entertainment/article/Tom-Graham-walks-every-street-in-San-Francisco-3182272.php.

Hamblin, Joan S., "Voyage of the "Brooklyn," *Ensign,* July 1997, pp. 16-19.

Johnson, Kenneth A., and Bartow, Greg W., eds., "San Francisco – Geology of the Cities of the World", Association Engineering Geologists, Sept. 16-22, https://www.aegweb.org>assets>docs>updated.

Kurutz, Gary F., "News from El Dorado: Newspapers and the California Gold Rush," International Federation of Library Associations and Institutions, 67th IFLA Council and General Conference, August 16-25, 2001, http://origin-archive.ifla.org>ifla67>papers.

Luce, W. Ray, "The Mormon Battalion: A Historical Accident?" *Utah Historical Quarterly*, vol. 42, no. 1, 1974, https://ISSUU.com>uhq>volume42_1974_number 1.

Peterson, Virgil V., "Early Mormon Journalism," *The Mississippi Valley Historical Review* (Oxford University Press), vol. 35, no. 4, March 1949.

Newspapers

Alta California.

The Californian.

The California Star.

The Friend, July 1, 1846.

The Polynesian, June 27, 1846.

New York Daily Tribune, Aug. 27, 1846.

New York Herald, Aug. 19, 1848.

New York Messenger, Nov. 15, 1845.

Sacramento Daily Union, Sept. 11, 1866.

Archival Sources

The Bancroft Library, University of California Berkeley.

Brigham Young Collection, LDS Archives, Brigham Young University.

California Digital Newspaper Collection, UCR Center for Bibliographical Studies and Research.

California History Room, California State Library, Sacramento CA; cslcal@library.ca.gov.

Von Langsdorff, Georg Heinrich, Voyages and Travels in Various Parts of the World during the years 1803, 1804, 1805, 1806 and 1807; London: Printed for Henry Colburn, 1814, in The Rezanov Voyage to Nueva California, The Russell California Reprints, San Francisco: Private Press of Thomas C. Russell, 1927.

San Francisco Historical Society, San Francisco CA.

The Society of California Pioneers, San Francisco CA.

Soule, Frank, Gihon, John H. and Nisbet, James, Annals of San Francisco. New York: D. Appleton & Co., 1855, in FoundSF, The San Francisco Digital Archive, https://www.foundsf.org.

Sutter's Fort State Historic Park, California Department of Parks and Recreation, Archives.SuttersFort@parks.ca.gov.

Miscellaneous

"California's Second Newspaper," Sacramento History Museum, tiktok, video, https://www.tiktok.com>video.

MacFarlane, Angus, "The Long and Twisted Road of How San Francisco Became San Francisco," San Francisco Historical Society Youtube presentation, July 13, 2022, https://www.youtube.com/c/SanFranciscoHistoricalSociety.

William Briggs

Marshall Gold Discovery State Historic Park, brochure, Gold Discovery Park Association, California State Parks.

Sutter's Fort State Historic Park, brochure, California State Parks.

www.ingramcontent.com/pod-product-compliance
Lightning Source LLC
Chambersburg PA
CBHW071319120626
46546CB00002B/378